GOURMET &
SPECIALTY SHOPS

GOURMET &
SPECIALTY SHOPS

Martin M. Pegler

Visual Reference Publications, Inc. ▪ New York

Visual Reference Publications
302 Fifth Avenue
New York, NY 10001

Distributors to the trade in the United States and Canada
Watson-Guptill Publishers
1515 Broadway
New York, NY 10036

Distributors outside the United Sates and Canada
HarperCollins International
10 E. 53rd Street
New York, NY 10022

Library of Congress Cataloging in Publication Data:
Gourmet & Specialty Shops
Printed in Hong Kong
ISBN 1–58471–052–7
Designed by Dutton & Sherman

CONTENTS

INTRODUCTION

Today's food shoppers—like fashion shoppers—are smarter, more sophisticated and much more aware of what is going on all over the world. They are also in a hurry—time poor—and want what they want when they want it. They are willing to pay the price but expect value and service—and they want selection.

The food marketing field has become "boutiqued." Specialty food stores are expected to carry an in-depth selection: the best brands and the best products from all around the globe. Gourmet shops may still be "precious" and "select" but they are facing serious competition from the shops-within-the-supermarkets. These "boutiques," in some of the better, more upscale markets, now show and sell the best, the finest and even the exotic, if that is what their shoppers expect. Companies that have established themselves over the decades selling their superior specialties through catalogues, are now setting up retail outlets or boutiques where they can showcase their wares and compete with the specialty stores by becoming one of them. Harry & Davis is one example of this phenomena.

Though it is over a decade since a generation was defined as the "Now Generation," Generations X and Y and maybe Z all want immediate gratification when it comes to food. In keep-ing with that, we are seeing small dine-in cafés appearing as attach-ments to Gourmet and Specialty stores. We have become acclimated to the coffee houses that have grown up around us as purveyors of prepack-aged or packed-to-order special blends and roasts of coffee. How do you know if you really like a particu-lar blend unless you taste it? If you can try a cup of a special blend, why not have a cookie, or a muffin, or maybe even a sandwich with it? Just as coffee shops are selling baked goods, bakeries now have small cafés added to their spaces.

Wine tasting and wine bars are now part of some better wine stores. Try it—and buy it! It is a rarity to find a market or supermarket that doesn't have an on-the-floor café where shop-pers can sample what is available. The new Petrossian Boutique and Fauchon—two of the most elegant of gourmet specialty food stores—have cafés for the immediate gratification of their affluent clientele. Home Meal Replacement (HMR) is big business catering to today's busy lifestyle and specialty stores, markets and super-markets are catering to this trend with more gourmet and upscale styled dishes—partially or fully prepared or even made-to-order—and ready to-go. And then again—why not sample before making a decision?

People are smarter and more aware. People are tuned in on the world and on themselves. Good Health and Living Longer and Better are the pursuits of many. We are see-ing bigger, better designed and more fully stocked natural foods and organically grown produce stores. There are still the small, crowded and tasteless coops selling to the health lifestyle converts, but even supermarkets are expanding their Natural Food boutiques and vitamin and food supplement areas and offering alternatives in bright, light, well designed spaces.

Gourmet and Specialty foods must lure, entice and ensnare shop-pers by appealing to all the senses: smell to make a selection; sight to reassure; touch—if allowed—to con-firm freshness; and taste to be con-vinced. Add to this color corrected lighting, complementary colors, pleas-ing textures, and the theater of chefs, cooks and food handling specialists at work in open-for-viewing prep areas and kitchens, and you have what it takes to please today's knowledgeable and demanding shoppers.

As you turn these pages you will find some interesting, some exciting, some novel and some traditional store design approaches to the visual presentation of fine foods. Something for everyone! I hope that you will find the variety of selections a visual treat as well as a worthwhile tour of gastrotomy today.

Martin M. Pegler

GOURMET &
SPECIALTY SHOPS

A.G.FERRARI FOODS
San Francisco, CA

Annibale Giovanni Ferrari, the founder of what is today A.G.Ferrari Foods spent his youth in the early years of the 20th century working in his family's "gastonomia"—specialty food store—in the Emilia Romagna region of Italy. By 1919, Annibale Giovanni, still in his teens, had emigrated to the U.S. and opened his first food store in the Bay area. Now, over 80 years later it is his grandson, Paul Ferrari, who is proud to be the keeper of the family tradition and the twelve stores in the San Francisco area that bear his grandfather's name.

In keeping with the ever-changing demands of an ever upscaling society, Paul Ferrari commissioned Landor

ARCHITECT/DESIGNER ◆ Landor Architects, San Francisco, CA
DESIGNERS ◆ Jean Loo/Matt Harvey/ Anastasia Laksmi/John Kiil
CREATIVE DIRECTOR ◆ Scott Drummond & Nicholas Aparicio
ART DIRECTOR ◆ Courtney Reeser
PHOTOGRAPHER ◆ Michael Friel & Cesar Rubio
FIXTURE CREDITS ◆ Fixture Credits

Architects of San Francisco, to create a new identity for the Italian specialty stores that were previously called Ultra Lucca. It was decided to go back to the name of the original founder and thus create an identity that "clearly expressed its (A.G. Ferrari Foods) heritage, company spirit, and passion for food in the authentic Italian tradition." In addition to the new name and logo, the Landor Architects designed a retail environment that reflects an authentic "gastronomia." It starts on the street where shoppers are greeted by the sunny, yellow-gold stucco finished facade and the attractive and attracting Pompeiian red awnings emblazoned with the new "antique" logo design of A.G. Ferrari Foods. Inside the store, the shopper is most pleasantly assailed by sights and smells that entice and bewitch. The store's interior palette of warm white plastered walls, simple gray concrete floors, white Carrera marble counters and assorted natural, light wood fixtures trimmed with stainless steel and glass sits back and allows the abundant and often overflowing display of gourmet treats to step forward in all their glorious colors and textures. In keeping with the old world Italian gastronomia tradition there are hand written price labels, chalk boards with specials and recommendations scrawled on them, natural wood crates, baskets and bushels to contain the plethora of specialties. As Martin Halle, the store manager said, "It's very Italian and the new look revolves around who we are—our heritage. I like the high ceilings and the warm color scheme and even the cement floor communicates that we are family stores." Adding to the family feeling are the framed black and white pictures of the Ferrari family hung on the creamy walls of members.

- Bread
Displayed
near the
cheese

Light enters through the large mullioned windows on two sides of the store and the ribbed, crystal domed pendants provide the ambient light. Along the perimeter walls track lights are added to illuminate the merchandise displayed on the walls and on the cases, crates and rustic containers lined up along with the counters. Overall the feeling is warm and sunny—as though the yellow glow from the exterior has seeped in and stained the interior.

Though the different areas of the store are specialized and more clearly defined there is still a feeling of warmth and friendliness that brings it all together. The shopper is invited to sample and select from a variety of cheeses and olives, wines, vinegars, oils, pastas, polenta, jarred vegetables and other Italian imported delicacies as well as fresh baked goods and a changing menu of freshly prepared appetizers, soups and entree to-go. In addition, the store is filled with a large selection of basics and specialty foods imported from Italy where the firm has its own buyers just outside of Florence. Weather permitting, small outdoor tables are provided under the comforting awnings where diners can enjoy dining on the foods available inside.

The *San Francisco Chronicle* has knighted Paul Ferrari, the CEO and taste palate behind A.G.Ferrari Foods, "The ambassador of all things Italian." Paul Ferrari said, "We are not going to change the pace of our lives but I think the Americans are yearning for the sort of meals the Italians have every day—healthy, simple and delicious. A.G. Ferrari Foods is my way of inviting you all to sit down at the table, have a great meal, have a glass of wine and enjoy life. As my grandfather always said, 'La qualita non ha tempo'—(Quality is Timeless)."

PETROSSIAN BOUTIQUE/CAFÉ
Seventh Ave., New York, NY

When you want "gourmet" you can't ask for more "gourmet" than Petrossian. The firm was founded in Paris in 1920 and has in the ensuing years established an enviable name and reputation around the world as purveyors of fine foods.

When a 1500 sq.ft. space opened up next to the Petrossian Restaurant on Seventh Ave. and 58th St. New York City, the company took it over for a Boutique/Café in which they could offer a selection of their caviars, smoked fishes, pates, fois gras, truffles, candies and imported packaged delicacies. These were previously available in a small retail corner of the restaurant. In addition, it was decided that the Café would also serve up fresh breads, pastries and baked-to-order desserts to go as well as prepared gourmet take-out food. David Schefer Design of New York was commissioned to prepare the elegant box in which the gourmet jewels would be offered.

Among the problems facing David Schefer's design team was integrating a working kitchen into an elegantly finished interior. The working kitchen was placed in front of the window so that passers-by could see

the action. The raw ingredients as well as the finished product are on view and the results are so tempting. "Simple and elegant materials were used to create the backdrop for Petrossian's renowned products," said David Schefer. Mahogany woodwork, carrera marble floors and counter tops, acid washed mirrors, a palladium leaf ceiling cove over the beige plaster walls and highlighting the beige ceiling, brass and glass detailing and leather upholstered furniture in the café all contribute to the richness of the setting.

DESIGNER ◆ David Schefer Design, New York, NY
PROJECT DESIGN TEAM ◆ David Schefer & Eve-Lynn Schoenstein
ARCHITECT OF RECORD ◆ Richard Lewis Architect
LIGHT CONSULTANT ◆ Hellmann Di Bernardo
LIGHTING SUPPLIERS ◆ Iris Downlights/Kurt Versen Wall Washers
MILLWORK & CABINETRY ◆ Designs by David Schefer Designs constructed by Bronx Builders
REFRIGERATED CASES ◆ David Schefer Design built by Bronx Builders
ROTISSERIES/OVENS ◆ David Schefner Design built by Bronx Builders
CHOCOLATE DISPLAY CASE ◆ Parisi/Royal, customized by Bronx Builders.
PHOTOGRAPHER ◆ David M. Joseph, New York, NY

Inside the store a central aisle was created and different merchandising areas are unified by a common display system and use of materials. The mahogany paneled perimeter walls are lined with shelving and product display surrounds the shopper. At the rear of the space, raised up on a carpeted mezzanine, is the intimate Café. Traditional materials such as mahogany, white carrera marble, crackle glazed tiles and alabaster light fixtures surround the cozy dining area. From here the diner is somewhat separated from the action on the selling floor yet still has a view of the scene. There is also maximum visibility from the street.

Lighting plays a very important part in the design of the space. In addition to well lit areas for product display and the kitchen prep area, the plan required "creating a warm and inviting interior suitable for elegant and upscale in-store dining." The designers provided recessed wall washers and under shelf lighting as well as decorative, antique lighting fixtures "to provide ambient lighting and visual interest." The final design provides "an accessible and attractive in-store dining without compromising the retail selling environment."

FAUCHON
Park Ave., New York, NY

Say the name "Fauchon" to any knowledgeable lover of fine foods and he or she will start to salivate. If there is a universally recognized "heaven" for gourmets it must have its address in Paris and it must have a sign proclaiming it as "Fauchon."

A new 3600 sq. ft. Fauchon has just opened in New York City at a distinguished address: Park Ave. and E. 56th St. Bognadow & Partners, of New York City, used just enough elements of the recently renovated Parisian store to suggest that Mecca of Fine Foods but still created a look that is distinctively its own. The space has been divided into two areas: a main sales floor that encircles a central kiosk where a knowledgeable sales staff is ready to assist and a tea salon with 40 seats at 14 tables. Along the 56th St. wall there are also staffed counters displaying teas, an epicerie case and assorted chocolate stations.

A yellowish Giallo Sabra marble, similar to the one in the Parisian store, covers the floor of the sales area. All cabinets, cases and mill-work—custom designed by Bogdanow & Partners—are made of curly maple wood. They feature "traditional details and a very high level of craftsmanship"—"straightforward and unfussy." The walls, ceiling and supporting columns are painted white and relieved by the wood detailing and the wrought iron curlrques—"a specifically Gaellic detail"—on the display units.

The visual presentation is exquisite as at the Paris address. The beautifully packaged jars, boxes and bags are set out on the shelves. Teas are stored in dark ornamental jars that

---

DESIGN ◆ Bogdanow & Partners, New York, NY
DESIGN TEAM ◆ Warren Ashworth/Keary Horiuchi/Tina Lai
CONTRACTOR ◆ Richter & Ratner, Maspeth, NY
MILLWORK & CABINETS ◆ Richter & Ratner, Maspeth, NY
REFRIGERATED CASES ◆ Federal
LIGHTING ◆ Edison Price
FLOORING ◆ Stone Source, New York, NY
FURNITURE ◆ Custom Fabricated for Fauchon
PHOTOGRAPHY ◆ Dub Rogers

are also functional. These jars are displayed on a curved, free standing wall/shelf unit that backs up the tea salon. Behind the jars, glass panels with laminating pieces of bronze fabrics between them, create "a wall shimmering with a bronze glow." The whole space is bright and well lit by the daylight that streams in through windows on two sides and the recessed lights in the ceiling.

The tea salon is filled with memories of the original Fauchon. There is an animated and lively mural on one wall painted by the same artist

who created the one in the Parisian salon. The same striped upholstery on a pair of meridian chaise longues, as in the Paris location, continues the resemblance as does the choice of tables and chairs.

Just as the tempting, mouth watering, eye-filling displays are a "must-see" in Paris, the windows on Park Ave. and on E. 56th St. are filled with gourmet masterpieces—ready to eat. One has only to enter the door under the awning that boldly proclaims "Fauchon" in its pink logotype—and try and buy.

FORTNUM & MASON
Piccadilly, London, UK

Not only does the Royal Family shop the red carpeted, elegantly wood paneled Food Hall at Fortnum & Mason, but so does anybody that wants and can afford the choicest and finest of gourmet foods, condiments, wines and gift items. The heritage of Great Britain is reflected in the floor that has been newly designed by Dula Werke of Dortmund working with Christopher Blackwell, head of Fortnum & Mason's design Department.

Starting as a stall in a Piccadilly doorway in 1707, Fortnum & Mason has grown to become "grocers and provision merchants to the Queen." It is an institution dedicated to gourmet food where fine foods and wines are elegantly presented amidst marble, fine woodworking, crystal chandeliers, gilt trim and fixtures that resemble finely finished furniture. Upon entering into the brilliantly lit and richly colored hall, the shopper has to be impressed by "the cultural images of the Food Hall and the wonderful variety of products offered." The floor is laid out as a series of interrelated boutiques or departments which are accessible and logical. On the perimeter walls, covered with 18th century style paneling and architectural details, there are decorative arched niches cut into the wall in which decorative friezes "illustrate" the various food classifications in "an inspiring style." These display areas are varied and amusing and done in the exquisite style that is the trademark of the store's display department headed by Christopher Blackwell.

DESIGN ◆ Dula Werke, Dortmund, Germany
Christopher Blackwell, Fortnum & Mason, Director of Display
FIXTURES & FITTINGS ◆ Designed and Manufactured by Dula, Dortmund
VISUAL MERCHANDISING & DISPLAY ◆ Christopher Blackwell and Staff
DECORATIVE ELEMENTS AND SPECIAL FURNITURE ◆ Selected by Christopher Blackwell

The floor treatment is an open and spacious one and even the mirror covered columns add to the feeling of spaciousness. In addition to the elegant crystal and brass hanging chandeliers, the space sparkles with warm and luxuriant light from the spots that line up along the cross beams of the coffered ceiling. The wood gondolas, out in the center of the red carpeted floor, are finished with half round end pieces that not only show off what is available but adds to ease of movement through the space. The rich mahogany wood used on the fixtures/fittings complements the paler wood applied to the perimeter walls. In some departments such as the wine shop and the fresh produce areas, the wood fixtures are whitewashed for a lighter look. Rustic wicker baskets coddle the assorted fruits and vegetables shown under the MR16 lamps and accented with green foliage. The fresh cut flowers and live plants are set adjacent to the select produce.

Blackwell brings his unique talents to this area by adding decorative seasonal elements and architectural props that upscale the already upscale product offering. The classic urn "fountain" in the center of the Food Hall is regularly changed to promote new arrivals, seasonal changes and holiday events.

MIZNER'S PROVISIONS
Boca Raton, FL

Blossoming in the Boca Raton Resort & Club, where a flower shop once stood, is the new Mizner's Provisions—an upscale yet casual marketplace in an elegant yet casual setting. The shop is located nearby and complements the existing Caffe Espresso as well as the central lobby courtyard. The shop was designed by Pavlik Design Team of Ft. Lauderdale and the design concept furthers the "timeless, romantic Mediterranean architectural style" that dominates in the Boca Raton Resort & Club.

The new space balances traditional styles and decorative motifs with the fast paced lifestyles of today. Mizner's product presentation features European pastries, an extensive line of private label coffees, chocolates and sweets, a selection of packaged teas, mustards, spices, oils and toppings along with an extensive selection of gourmet gift items and cook books. To accommodate the variety of product and yet maintain the "open, casual look" of the surroundings, the Pavlik Team used distressed woods, scrolled iron work, and intricate mosaic tilework "to evoke an historical quality" which is updated with contemporary overtones evident through the extensive use of hand painted, faux finished walls. The sun-drenched, ocher wall finish, the light, natural wood floor and the provincial, rustic-style tables all contribute to the Mediterranean ambiance of the shop The repeated arch openings—like a portico—also adds to the outdoor feeling of the space. The stamped metal ceiling, overhead, has been painted a warm,

DESIGN ◆ Pavlik Design Team, Ft. Lauderdale, FL
DESIGN TEAM ◆ Ronald J. Pavlik, CEO
  Brent Cartwright
PROJECT MANAGER & DESIGNER ◆ Sven Pavlik:
PHOTOGRAPHY ◆ Marina Larenz, Ft.
  Lauderdale, FL

dark brown color which is high-lighted by a square of deep terra cotta. The dark color is recalled on the floor by the deep, mahogany col-ored cases, counters and the slim etageres spaced between the open arches. The shop's name is embed-ded in the mosaic tile design that adorns the dark wood entablature surrounding the wall cubicles that feature pre-packaged foods.

Hanging from the terra cotta ceil-ing squares are half-round, white alabaster bowls caught in a web of wrought iron tracery. These lighting fixtures provide the ambient light

while tracklights equipped with focusable lamps illuminate the mer-chandise displayed on the wall units and the floor fixtures and tables. During the daylight hours light streams in from the patio garden area.

Mizner's Provisions gourmet shop has "proven to be a major suc-cess in aesthetic enhancement of the historic resort" while providing food delicacies and gift items of food for the upscale clientele.

DEAN & DELUCA MARKET/CAFÉ
Charlotte, NC

When a connoisseur of fine foods is asked to list culinary havens in New York City, one can bet that the Dean & De Luca Market on Broadway & Prince St. will make the list along with Balducci's and the two newcomers; Petrossian and Fauchon. However, when Dean & De Luca decided to open up in the Charlotte, NC area, they turned to local designers, Little & Associates, to develop a new concept for this specialty food retailer.

The 4000 sq. ft. satellite Market Café is a specialty prepared food store and the concept allows Dean & De Luca to reach customers in a

broad geographic area without having to duplicate the complexity or cost of its main stores which are usually about 12,000 sq.ft. in size. The Market Café is actually an outpost that offers fresh foods that are prepared in the main Dean & De Luca store in Charlotte and then delivered fresh each morning to the outlying Market Cafés. Each main store services three to four satellites. All the ingredients that go into the preparation of the prepared foods are displayed in a way that suggests that the foods have been prepared on site. All of this reinforces the sense of freshness to the shopper.

The space is filled with light and the colors are neutral. Tall windows fill three sides of the store and the high ceiling is painted the same, warm, creamy color as the walls. These contrast with the dark maple moldings around the windows and door as well as the tables and chairs set out in the café area. The floor is concrete tinted and scored to look like large baked terra cotta tiles. The metal industrial shelving racks that carry the prepackaged foods out on the floor and along some of the perimeter walls also recall the prep areas in fine gourmet restaurants while they also add a glint of silvery sheen to the wood and painted space. Stainless steel cases are used to house the prepared-to-go foods,

salads, and such. Glass covers and sneeze guards add another light touch. To supplement the daylight there are halide lamps set in the glossy white metal shades of the drop lights. Spots are set into the ceiling over the fresh foods area as well as in the track lights lined up on the exposed ceiling. The giant HVAC duct swings around overhead and its silvery metal finish goes with the metal stacking units standing beneath it. "The Market Café's neutral materials and finishes and subtle signing puts food on center stage."

DESIGN ◆ Little & Associates, Charlotte, NC
DESIGN TEAM ◆ Steven Starr: Senior Designer & Project Manager
  Josh Cool and Scott Frazier
SHELVING UNITS ◆ Metro Shelving
KITCHEN EQUIPMENT ◆ Foodkraft, Winston Salem, NC
GENERAL CONTRACTOR ◆ J.B. Waddell, Charlotte, NC
LIGHTING ◆ Juno, Des Plaines, IL. & Spero, Cleveland, OH
CONCRETE FLOOR ◆ L.M. Schofield Products, Douglasville, GA
PLUMBING/MECHANICAL/ELECTRICAL ◆ Clive Samuels & Assoc., Princeton, NJ
FURNITURE ◆ Falcon
PHOTOGRAPHY ◆ Stanley Capps

TUSCANY PIZZA MARKET
King of Prussia, PA

Located in the upscale King of Prussia Mall in the city of the same name is this unusual gourmet specialty food shop/pizzeria. An incredible array of gourmet pastas and pizzas as well as prepared and pre-packaged Italian food specialties are available for dining-in in a charming setting or for take-out. A well stocked food service line attracts the shopper. He or she can select from indulgences such as imported delicacies, freshly baked breads and pastries and unique prepared foods to garden fresh fruits and vegetables in an impressive market area.

Designed by Gary Aldridge & Associates of Atlanta, GA, the open for viewing and entering shopfront creates an environment that "evokes the warmth, flavor and refined elegance of the Italian countryside." The sweeping curve of the entrance is underlined by the green ceramic tiles underfoot at the mall line and the bowed soffit above accented with the green tiles. To one side, behind a pseudo Tuscan facade and pediment, is the market area with products displayed in glass cases between the square, Ionic trimmed columns. Atop bushels and baskets, gaily stained red, white and green, fresh produce is on display. To the left of the main, central aisle—marked off with off-white ceramic tiles—is the Pizzeria and the lavish presentation of prepared pastas, pizzas and entrees to-go or to-stay.

A giant wood trellis, stained a dark color, is suspended over the beige tiled floor and the trellis is trimmed with multi-colored streamers. Round tables of natural wood support elevated displays of packaged food products while striped wood baskets, on the floor, encircle

DESIGNER ◆ Gary Aldridge & Associates, Atlanta, GA
ARCHITECT ◆ John Walker, AIA, Philadelphia. PA
OWNER ◆ Siganos Management, Northfield, NJ
PHOTOGRAPHY ◆ Martin Photography, Inc., Northfield, NJ

the tables. They carry more of the fresh fruits, vegetables and breads. Behind gondolas of a rich mahogany color that make a swing through the space, is a colonnade of crenelated, Ionic capped columns that support a matching curved entablature. Here, tables are set up for diners under an illuminated, faux painted blue sky. The walls are "washed" with earthy colors to simulate a loose, watercolor-like rendition of a Tuscan village streetscape. Throughout, the designer has imbued the scene with the flavor and culture of Old Italy—or at least as we would like to think of it.

29

FALORNI
Greve, Italy

Forty minutes and only about 30 kilometers out of Florence is the small, laid-back town of Greve. Located in the heart of the Chianti country, the old town boasts a main square that seems to be an old Hollywood stage set. The pair of embracing colonnades to either side of the central cobblestoned area are filled with small specialty shops mostly vending bottled and packaged specialties of the area. In this seemingly sleepy town with its centuries old buildings, colors faded from the sun, and snuggled into one of the cool arcades, is the noted specialty store, Falorni's Salumi. People travel from all over Italy for the salamis, hams and sausages available here.

DESIGN • The owners of Falorni
PHOTOGRAPHY • MMP/RVC

A stuffed boar greets shoppers outside the all-glass door through which one gets a first look at the inviting shop. Once inside, besides the heady aroma that makes just breathing a gastronomic experience, there is the overwhelming sight of the many salamis and cured hams. They hang from the ancient timber rafters that cross over the store which is made up of a series of rooms. The salamis hang from hooks protruding off the stained wood moldings that circle and band the white-washed, textured plaster walls and they overflow off the large and small unmatched rustic tables that serve as floor displayers. The shopper is encouraged to taste the wares and there is always someone—wrapped in a large, white butcher's apron—there to guide the novice in his/her introduction to the wonders of the many different products to be found in this salami/sausage showroom in Greve. It's a slice of salami here—a snippet of cheese there—and then in

the very back room a wine tasting table where one can sample the distilled fruits of the local vineyards.

Rustic is the theme and rustic is the palette of materials and colors. Up front, the floors are covered in a varied pattern of broken bits and pieces of local granite and stones that range from gray and beige to rust and black. As one steps farther into the shop, the flooring varies from room to room. In some, gray green granite

tiles are laid in an orderly pattern and some are covered with concrete. In other rooms the original heavy, dark brown timber floors are still evident. The changing floor materials actually help to delineate the areas and the products in them.

Fresh meats are stored in glistening, stainless steel refrigerated cases up near the entrance to the store. Adjacent to the fresh meats are small salamis set out in woven baskets on

beds of straw. Throughout, rough woven baskets of wicker and twigs, wood crates and small tables of stained wood are used to highlight the products as well as provide the desired provincial, fresh-from-the-farm ambiance.

It is like the sign out front says—For Sale, Salamis, Typical of Greve in Chianti. That is an understatement: it is really a gourmet's heaven in a delightful, rustic setting.

HARRY & DAVID
West Farms Mall, Farmington, CT

For over 75 years the name "Harry & David" has been associated with holiday gifts of quality and gourmet food items usually purchased from catalogs. Traditionally seen as a "fourth quarter" holiday business with gift boxes and baskets sent all over the country, management decided to make Harry & David "a year round treat and an anytime of the year source for gifts." With this in mind, JGA, Inc. (Jon Greenberg & Associates) of Southfield, MI was called upon to create the "in-store communication."

The target market is 30 years and older women with discretionary income who are interested in high quality, unique food and serving merchandise as well as any shopper interested in gourmet food gifts for corporate accounts.

To make shopping Harry & David an "experience of discovery and efficiency," the 4350 sq. ft. space is laid out as a series of shops: candy and snack shop, gourmet food shop, holiday trends, home entertaining and the gift basket shop. All the cues and codes of food, its preparation, presentation and consumption are evident as the underlying theme for the space. Customers can select their own special assortment from the array of chilled Harry & David produce and gifts in the walk-in cooler. Through the use of tables and hutches, "the store becomes the kitchen, the buffet, the dining room table that we all dream of." The

DESIGN ◆ JGA, Inc. (Jon Greenberg & Associates), Southfield, MI
DESIGN TEAM ◆ Ken Nisch: Chairman
Kathi McWilliams: Creative Director
Skip West: Studio Director
Katie Shaieb: Senior Designer
Mike McCahill: Project Manager
Wendi Knape: Design
Stephanie Gach: Color & Materials Specialist
Charles Dunlap: Resource Specialist
CLIENT'S TEAM ◆ Bearcreek Corp., Medford, OR
Paul Schleisinger: VP of Operations
Carl Horn Davis: Director of Store Planning
Michael Gebert: Director of V.M.
ARCHITECT ◆ J. Michael Kirk, AIA, Southfield, MI
GENERAL CONTRACTOR ◆ Fisher Development, Inc., San Francisco, CA
MILLWORK & WOOD FIXTURES ◆ CRW Inc., Lincoln, NE
METAL FIXTURES ◆ Hampton Lane, Glendale, CA
LIGHTING CONSULTANT ◆ Illuminating Concepts, Farmington Hills, MI
PHOTOGRAPHY ◆ Laszlo Regos Photography, Berkley, MI

company's northwest roots are realized in the "northwest contemporary" architecture which is warm and friendly and just as evident is the company's sense of tradition.

"Craft and style with a casual interpretation is found throughout the space" which is rich in natural materials, colors and textures. Natural slate, cherry, limed wood finishes and metal are used to affect "an environment of style without pretension." A greenhouse is suggested by the glass wall exterior with the charcoal gray window framing and the natural slate trim. The soft green palette that is used complements Harry & David's Riviera pears. The set perimeter fixtures contrast with the curved, residential-like feel of the cherry and pale limed oak fixtures that are used to create the easy traffic flow around the store. Special finishes and focal points such as the "Tower of Treats" fixture that replicates the firm's renowned food gifts make the tour an enjoyable experience. The store design and the in-store communication "combine to create a veritable feast, even relying on scaled up serving elements and pieces to hold product."

MUSTARD SEED MARKET
Solon, OH

Phillip and Margaret Nabors, through their Mustard Seed Market and Café, have established themselves as northern Ohio's leading gourmet and certified organic food supplier. According to Margaret Nabors, "I am the mom in a mom and pop business who loves our customers, our team members and our children. As mom, I consider it my duty to protect the integrity of the food we serve and those we love. Our ingredient standards assure our customers that they will find clean food under our roof."

This, the Solon store, is the second store and the designers, Jerry Herschman & Stuart Berger of Herschman Architects of Beachwood,

DESIGN ◆ Herschman Architects, Beachwood, OH
DESIGN TEAM ◆ Jerry Herschman & Stuart Berger
PHOTOGRAPHY ◆ Kevin Reeves

OH, had to make this space express to entering shoppers that this is the place where the philosophy of food and healthy living are of the greatest importance. Like the original store, the new design "enhances the retail food store aesthetic and incorporates the expansion of services in the new food market experience." The two-level space consists of a simple palette of colors and materials that "create the dynamic yet unifying patterns and textures which define the market." The various departments are integrated with the cherry wood and machined steel trimmed fixtures on the aisles. There are also visually impressive perimeter service cases of black combined with stainless steel. The gray green and light gray VCT floor tiles, laid in a checkerboard pattern, "shifts scale and orientation to define the market departments for the shoppers." Establishing harmony and unifying the space is the wall pattern created by balancing open areas painted white with cherry colored wood grids and fascia strips that wrap around the interior walls. In the preparation and cooking kitchens the white ceramic tiled walls are patterned with bands of black and white checkerboarded tiles. Sitting in front of these walls are the stainless steel kitchen equipment, the cooking units and the exhaust hoods. Altogether they create an image that bespeaks of cleanliness.

"Custom flat cut cherry millwork accented with stainless steel edges enhances the harmony and creates a warm tone throughout the market and the restaurant." Three dimensional stainless steel faced letters are used for the departmental identities. The first level of the store features the gourmet and organic food market, the Natural Living department and the Market Kitchen where the specialty take-out foods are prepared. On the second level there is a restaurant with its own kitchen, a banquet room, meeting and conference rooms, a demo kitchen for the cooking school and corporate offices. Lighting up the space was a very important part of the design. In the Market area, the high exposed corrugated ceiling and all the pipes and ducts running through it are painted white. Commercial type halogen lights hang down to provide

light levels necessary without calling attention to themselves. The perimeter shops, tucked away under the mezzanine, have warmer lighting units to enhance the food products. The dropped ceiling on the second, or mezzanine level, is equipped with recessed incandescent lamps and some halogen lamps.

The new Mustard Seed is becoming a home away from home for the health conscious shopper/diner. As Margaret Nabors says, "If you come to our home you will see the store. This is how we live—taking responsibility for our family's and our customer's health and wellbeing."

NATURE'S NORTHWEST
Lake Oswego, Portland, OR

The design objective for JGA, Inc. (Jon Greenberg & Associates), Southfield, MI was to "create an eclectic and visually stimulating environment" in the 42,000 sq. ft. space that would express Nature's Northwest "way of life." The design had to reflect a healthy lifestyle and reinforce the company's brand by integrating Nature's diverse mix of natural foods and groceries, specialty foods, a deli/café, pharmacy/nutrition department, salon and spa, exercise and health education center and floral and gifts areas.

Taking their inspiration from the farmer's markets and marketplaces—spaces that create a sense of community—JGA Inc.'s design team created this unique shopping experience in Lake Oswego, just outside of Portland, OR. Up front, near the main entrance, is the loading dock so that shoppers can see the fresh produce and products being delivered. The market hall entrance opens onto "shops along the street" that invite shoppers to enter into and linger awhile. Departments that rely on convenient and efficient shopping patterns were grouped

together, identified, and organized with architectural and/or structural elements. To express the Nature's Northwest brand message and idea of "walk lightly on the earth," the designers specified simple and honest materials and visually stimulating colors presented within an "artisan crafted" look. Recycled materials, natural finished metals and hand crafted artisan fixtures are mixed with industrial and service equipment to "create a sense of efficiency and fun." The heavy timber supports and the timber ceiling structure all add to the farmer's market ambiance

as well as the real and natural feel of the space. A varied palette of environmental graphics, murals, and posters provide much of the decor. Props are used when they enhance the "close to the source" experience or when "a sense of whimsy was needed for its entertainment value."

To expedite and for the shopper's convenience, the store is laid out in a series of "trails" which accommodate the shopper's need- and time schedule. For the "adventure shopper" the way leads to discovery and a spontaneity of shopping, where the frequent shopper's

CREDITS ◆ JGA, Inc. (Jon Greenberg & Associates), Southfield, MI

DESIGN TEAM ◆ Ken Nisch, Chairman
Julie Sabourin

DIRECTOR OF CLIENT STRATEGY ◆ Kathi McWilliams

CREATIVE DIRECTOR ◆ Brian Hurttienne:
Project Manager
Mike Benincasa: Senior Designer

STAINED CONCRETE FLOORS ◆ Scofield Products & Ardex

WOOD FLOORS ◆ Custom Maple Floors

CORK FLOORS ◆ Natural Cork Ltd., Co.

PLANK FLOOR ◆ Permagrain Products, Inc.

CARPET ◆ Patoraft & Lee's Custom Carpets

TILE ◆ Ann Sacks, Portland OR/Pratt & Larsen, Portland,OR/ Dal Tile, Dallas, TX

PHOTOGRAPHY ◆ Charles Chestnut, Visual Aspect Photographers, Portland, OR

"trail" is the efficient and easy one to follow. Standard grocery and bulk food items are set out on natural wood finished gondolas in the center of the store. The specialty shops surround this core. There is a specialty cheese area, wine shop, tea department, soup "salad" bar, beverage bar and a popular "What's For Dinner?" shop where prepared foods are ready-to-go. A resident chef is there to advise and assist in healthy meal planning. The Home Replacement Meals (HRM) are located just inside the store entrance so that shoppers who are in a hurry for a quick pick-up meal that just needs tossing or heating can pick up

what they want and not waste time wandering throughout the rest of the store. According to Ken Nisch, CEO of JGA, Inc., "Nature's wants to be a place where people shop every week. They take the position that customers should make their own food decisions but the store should offer the opportunity to chose alternative products or traditional ones."

The 8000 sq.ft. mezzanine level is where the salon and spa are located as well as the self care center and Nature's Info Com. Interactive kiosks give shoppers access to the internet. CD Roms and videos on health and environmental concerns can be borrowed or purchased in the Info center. Local news events are posted on matrix boards in the

check-out area and on giant video screens. In the Produce section shoppers can see and hear interviews with farmers, growers and specialists on health and nutrition. "The store offers a sense of authenticity where a blend of community neighborliness and convenience serve well to create value in the customer's mind."

NATURE UNLIMITED
Raintree, NJ

What was once part of a traditional supermarket has been upscaled and specialized to show off a new food concept. To create the new look for the 6700 sq.ft. natural foods market in Raintree, NJ, the owner, Jerry Norkus, invited Gary Lind of Lind Design International of College Point, NY to design the store we now see.

There are two entrances into the store. One is directly from the street and the other is through an opening leading from the larger supermarket. The bold checkered tile floor at the latter entrance invites the supermarket shopper to venture forth and see what's new. Two produce cases are angled, at this point, to facilitate easy access. A profusion of foliage grows out of the forward sweep of the dropped ceiling and it appears to be supported by the large laminated bull-nose column/display unit. Once past the red and beige patterned floor the shopper steps into a sea of teal blue flooring and gently " floats" from one natural food area to the next. Each display case and/or freezer is topped with easy to see, easy to read signs. Throughout, the design team tried to create a "natural feeling" that would go well with the name and the organically grown produce. Ochers, beiges, bright greens and accents of paprika abound from the VCT floor tiles, the walls covered with curry fiber and wheat fiber wallcoverings to the accent laminates on the cases and the gondolas. According to Gary Lind, "We tried to create a light, natural and easy to shop feeling" for Nature Unlimited.

In addition to the fresh produce and the packaged natural foods there is an extensive area devoted to vitamins and health food supplements. The dark stained wood fascia and crown molding are separated by

a rich ocher wallcovering and the floor, here, is a rust color that contrasts with the black laminate accents on the gondolas. A small bookshop with a couch has been set aside at the rear of the space for those who need or want a quiet respite from shopping or just want more information about health related subjects. For those who want

a quick, healthy snack there is a salad bar up near the entrance from the supermarket as well as several tables for dine-ins.

Overhead signage in ocher, green and white assists shoppers through the space while gondola and case toppers in black, red and white provide the necessary point of sale information.

DESIGN ◆ Lind Design International, College
Point, NY

DESIGN TEAM ◆ Gary Lind/Steve Norkus/Bob
Jackey

ARCHITECT ◆ Jim Hoffman

ENGINEERS ◆ Tom Donnelly

LIGHTING ◆ Don Cantor, Lightsystems
Technology

MILLWORK & CABINETRY ◆ Lind Design Intl.

REFRIGERATED CASES ◆ Hill Refrigeration

PHOTOGRAPHY ◆ Gary Lind, Lind Design Intl.

LOTTE CHAMSIL
Seoul, Korea

In keeping with the Asian department store concept of using the basement levels for supermarkets, Pavlik Design Team of Ft. Lauderdale responded to the challenge from the Lotte Group to design a new look for their Lotte Chamsil store. Part of the challenge was what to do about the low ceilings, the seven foot diameter columns and how to respond to the access from two subway entries, two sets of escalators and the elevator banks that link the food department with the rest of the department store.

The designers came up with "dynamic forms that define the circulation and also add a sense of excitement." Though the color scheme is neutral it is also subtly dramatic as it plays white floors

and walls with floor fixtures that are either white trimmed with black or veneered with light natural wood and outlined in black. The black granite ledges around all the table fixtures—unusual in food presentation—does accentuate the colors of the produce and the packaged goods. On some of the specialty food counters like Candy and Packaged Condiments, Tea, etc., the black band appears at the base of the light natural wood counter and thus creates a strong impact against the light colored floor. Some departments or zones are accented by different floor colors or the introduction of stripes of contrasting colors such as the burgundy floor in Fresh Foods and the beige floor stripes near Chocolates. In the Produce section the swirling graphic inlay pattern of the floor is repeated overhead. "Due to the volume of shoppers daily, floor patterns are reflected onto ceilings to identify departments during very crowded business hours." The

problematic extra wide columns are covered with the light wood veneer and become anchors for the departments in the market. In the meat and fresh fish deppartments the white tiled walls are polka dotted with small black tiles and in the long dining area with the extra long service line, gray stripes interrupt the white floor tiles to create a wider look in the space. The graphics on the overhead disks, over the individual stations in the service line, graphically explain which foods are served where.

Throughout, the signage in both English and Korean script is readily seen. For quick recognition, the black suspended signs are surrounded by graphic artwork that identifies the project making the written word almost unnecessary. Horizontal banners hang off columns and piers and add additional accents of color as well as support store promotions. In the produce area giant photographic images decorate the frieze over the fruits and vegetables with reproductions of what is available beneath. Similar photographic images, printed on plastic panels that are lit from behind, create glowing crowns around the fresh foods area. Watery turquoise waves envelop the fresh fish area.

"The overall marketing message is ease of shopping and convenience, vast product selection and freshness in a clean, organized environment."

DESIGNER ◆ Pavlik Design Team, Ft. Lauderdale, FL
DESIGN TEAM ◆ Ronald J. Pavlik, President/CEO
Serif Ayad
DIRECTOR ◆ Patrricia Dominguez: Project Designer
Young Rock Park: Project Designer
GINA KIM ◆ Project Manager
SVEN PAVLEK ◆ Director of Lighting

SEIBU OH! GOURMET
Tokyo, Japan

Traditionally Japanese department stores have large supermarkets located below street level in their stores. Seibu's goal with Oh! Gourmet was "to create a gourmet and specialty food center with a gift and special occasion orientation." To accomplish this, Seibu called upon Callison Architecture, Inc. of Seattle to design the new space viewed here.

Instead of a basement level, Oh! Gourmet has been given prominence with a first floor location and the designers, working with the design team of Seibu Department Stores, used a visual merchandising strategy of engaging the shopper's senses of

smell, taste and sight. This was accomplished and it does bring shoppers to the new destination zone. To get the shopper involved and move her/him through the space, "tasting" or "sampling" points were established where the shopper can "experience the quality and freshness of the prepared foods." These points were established on an axis with major sight lines of the floor. Customers can readily identify the zones by the decorative blue lamps that highlight these focal spots. Another focal area is the wall at the escalator which was designed with flexible, modular cubbies. The cubbies are individually illuminated

and are identified with the Oh! Gourmet logo etched onto the frosted glass. Featured and promotional merchandise is presented in the small cubicles and special events are also situated in front of them.

Imported wines are becoming more and more popular in Japan and upscale patrons are looking for a selection when they shop. Oh! Gourmet features a wine shop with custom designed fixtures that carry point of sale brand and rating information. This makes the shopper more comfortable about making a selection.

The warm beige and light natural wood setting is illuminated with

DESIGN ◆ Callison Architecture Inc., Seattle, WA
DESIGN TEAM ◆ Paula Stafford: Principal in
    Charge of Store Design & V.M.
    Dawn Clark: Project Manager
    Elizabeth Buxton: Interior Design Director
CLIENT'S DESIGN TEAM ◆ Seibu Dept. Stores,
    Tokyo, Japan
    Masao Fujikawa: General Manager,
    Design & Planning Division
    Toshiaki Matsuhashi: Chief Manager,
    Environment & Space Store Planning
    Mari Tahira: Store Environment & Store
    Planning, V.M.
VISUAL MERCHANDISING CONSULTANT
    ◆ Catherine Van Dijk, Henderson, NE
SUPPLIERS/FABRICATORS/FIXTURES &
    DECORATIVES: ◆ Yoshichyo Co. Kyoto/Seven
    Continents, Toronto, ON/Silvestri, Los
    Angeles, CA/Christine Taylor Collection,
    Doylestown, PA/Omaha Store Interior
    Fixtures, Markham, ON/Iron Design
    Center, Seattle, WA/Hanger Corp.,
    Cowoga Park, CA/Bay Area Display, San
    Francisco, CA/The Mercier Group, Los
    Angeles, CA/Clark Horton, Santa Fe,
    NM/Palecek, Richmond, CA/David Smith
    & Co. Antiques, Seattle, WA/Storeworks,
    Eden Prairie, MN/Endo Light Corp.,
    Osaka/Resolute & HRS Designs, Seattle,
    WA

recessed fluorescents and recessed can spots along with the aforementioned hanging blue lamps. Baskets, brightly colored glass bottles and jars, are combined with terra cotta and iron and wire decorative elements throughout the space. In addition, the selling area is enlivened with assorted merchandising "stories" such as visually tempting presentations of condiments stacked with shelf art and photos, and an Italian theme used to show off a selection of imported pastas, wines, sauces, cheeses and bread in a shop-within-the-shop area.

GOURMET SATISFACTION
Iwataya Z-Side, Fukuoka, Japan

The prize winning Iwataya Z-Side Department Store is located in Fukuoka, Japan which is a major cultural and commercial center located on the busy Tsushima Strait and it is criss-crossed by numerous canals. The nine story department store was designed by Walker Group/CNI of New York to complement the flagship store. The concept for Iwataya Z-Side is a "total lifestyle environment."

Each floor has its own graphic identity and represents a specific lifestyle and the private brand labels and branded shops all focus on specific merchandise categories. The basic concept is carried over to the basement level where the food specialties and gourmet food and drink products are displayed for com-

muters and specialty shoppers rushing to and from the nearby train station.

The low ceilings provide an intimate scale to the food floor which is almost totally cream colored. The light marble and ceramic tiled floors are complemented by the light, natural wood cabinets, cases, shelves and wall units. Running along the ceiling are black, wrought iron decorative elements that add a Japanese architectural quality to the design. The massive square columns that support the nine floors above are all covered with large squares of ceramic tile and the columns are integrated into the total design scheme. Some become the core of four sided "shops" on the floor while others are accented with natural

wood shelves that support displays of the merchandise featured on the counters and cases below or around the column. Longer shelves connect the columns on the floor and provide additional display space above eye level.

Black is the accent color. It appears in the overhead metal work; it appears in the accent tile squares that break up the creamy floors with patterns or borders. Much of the metalwork is also finished in black to accentuate the vertical and horizontal lines of the design. A rich burgundy color appears as an accent color in some areas on soffits and in the signage. It is quite apparent in the burgundy and white mini-canvas

awnings that define the curved front of the Gourmet Bakery and it also highlights the light wood and white of the Cream Land Z-Café.

The Wine area gets a special wall treatment with pseudo stone arches outlining the angled wine bottles displayed on the illuminated shelves. On the deeper beige floor that delineates this area are metal wine displayers that repeat the motif of the wrought iron ceiling spanners, as well as deep wood "stacking boxes" which create an up front display for the featured wines. The boutique is softly illuminated by recessed spots and fluorescent fixtures while halide lamps in ribbed crystal shades hang over the aisles.

DESIGNER • Walker Group/CNI, New York, NY

ZEHNDER'S MARKETPLACE
Frankenmuth, MI

For over 100 years the Zehnder name has stood for good taste and quality in family dining. The objective set for JGA, Inc. (Jon Greenberg & Associates) of Southfield, MI was to convert the lower level of the well known restaurant into "a branded, contemporary, interactive food concept with highly visible chefs and bakers to portray a fresh quality image." The appeal was to be to the younger shoppers who might not usually frequent the restaurant but still, because of time constraints, look for home-style, cooked meals ready-to-go or who might prefer a less formal dining experience in the Z-Chef Café.

"Over the past three years our team of managers, chefs, architects and design consultants have worked to develop a new dining experience for Zehnder's," said Albert Zehnder, president of Zehnder's of Frankenmuth. "Our goal was to update and create an environment that complemented our 'old world' tradition with new and exciting food and retail presentation." The result is the new Marketplace which provides a European gourmet atmosphere—"without a pretentious feel." Leading shoppers through the open plan of the 7000 sq.ft. space are fun environmental graphics featuring Z-branding. A Tuscan-inspired palette of earthtones which includes mustard, rust and teal is used and it is accented by planked barn-like wood floor strips and concrete floor in the dining area. This sets the Z-Café apart from the Bakery and Gift areas of the Marketplace. A mosaic wall consisting of custom "vegetable" tiles highlights the entrance to the food line. Hanging from the exposed ceiling are custom designed, dramatic six foot

DESIGNER ◆ JGA, Inc. (Jon Greenberg & Associates), Southfield, MI
DESIGN TEAM ◆ Michael Crosson, CEO
Michael Benincasa: Sr. Designer
Brian Eastman: Graphic Design Director
Jeri Bademian-Elsie: Color & Materials Specialist
Stephanie Gach: Color & Materials Manager
John Cochran: Draftsperson
CLIENT'S DESIGN TEAM ◆ Zehnder's, Frankenmuth, MI
Al Zehnder: President
Bill Parlberg: V.P. Restaurant
Dee Zehnder: Retail Division Manager
John Zehnder: Food & Beverage Director
ARCHITECTURAL FIRM ◆ Daniel Walter, Frankenmuth, MI
GENERAL CONTRACTOR ◆ Maurer & Rausch Construction, Frankenmuth, MI
MILLWORK ◆ Warner Door, Frankenmuth, MI
FOOD SHOWCASES/DISPLAYERS ◆ Wescho, West Chester, PA
LIGHTING CONSULTANT ◆ Illuminating Concepts, Farmington Hills, MI
CUSTOM LIGHTS & METAL WORK ◆ Steve Frank Studio, Detroit, MI
SIGNS & GRAPHICS ◆ Swartz Graphics, Frankenmuth, MI
FURNITURE ◆ Tables & Chairs: Falcon
TILE ◆ Ann Sacks Tile & Stone/Dal Tile
VISUAL PROPS ◆ Hubert
FLOORS ◆ Wonderworks of America/DLW Scala
PHOTOGRAPHY ◆ Laszlo Regos Photography, Berkley, MI

copper chandeliers that illuminate the Café. The chandeliers are emblazoned with the signature Zehnder "Z" and enhanced by colorful stones and silverware. Copper "Z"s are sculpted into the silver and wrought iron railing that surrounds the Café.

"The Marketplace's open floor plan marche concept speaks to each of the senses: its sights, sounds, smells and feel create both a physical and visual taste treat for guests," says Michael Crosson, JGA's CEO. "We wanted to create a sense of energy and excitement for Zehnder's that was more about a food experience than eating." Visitors can see the food being prepared in the open kitchen and make their selections at the various "made to order" stations: Z-Soup, Z-Pizza, Z-Hot Stuff, Z-Pasta, Z-Salad, Z-Sandwiches and Z-Carvery. There are usually more than

30 items prepared fresh daily for take-home or eat-in in the adjacent 100 seat Café. In addition, the space interweaves culinary and gift merchandise.

The branding design, by JGA, Inc., sets the fun and light attitude that not only affects the design but appeals to the desired target market. The graphic Z-Chef became the main feature that gives Zehnder's and the Marketplace an "unpretentious European Gourmet" ambiance. Zehnder's is a "work in progress." Michael Crosson says, "Recognizing that the restaurant market is changing all the time, both the Zehnders and our firm feel that the whole facility has to be seen as a program of constant rebirth. Every area, whether merchandising, decor or renovation, is constantly being re-evaluated."

NEW YASMEEN BAKERY
Dearborn, MI

Situated in a middle income, residential area of Dearborn, MI is the newly remodeled New Yasmeen Bakery which is much more than its name implies. Catering to an ethnic and professional clientele, the 5300 sq. ft. space not only is an active bakery but also puts emphasis on specialty foods freshly prepared and ready-to-go. Marco Design Group of Northville, MI was commissioned to remodel the existing bakery/restaurant and create "an upscale, sophisticated, not ostentatious specialty food store offering high quality and value."

To appeal to the ethnic and local clientele, the designers adopted a strong Mediterranean theme and used a rich palette filled with sun

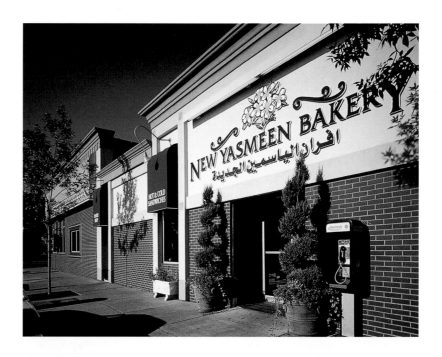

drenched yellow ocher combined and contrasting with various hues of blue. Added to this are the textures of the Mediterranean area and thus there is an extensive use of mosaics, ceramic tiles, brick and faux finishes highlighted by multi-colored, hand blown glass accent lights over the register locations.

In order to achieve an interior design scheme that would work in conjunction with the layout and also integrate the merchandising, architecture and environment into a satisfying shopping experience, certain changes were made. The old garage door was

transformed into a storefront window which exposes the interior to the street traffic. The designers created a "progression of experiences" that moves the shoppers through room-like settings as they wander from the pastry, bakery, deli, prepared foods and dining areas to culminate in the outdoor patio. Along the way the shopper is attracted by or amused by handpainted murals that capture the Mediterranean lifestyle; a series of painted images showing how pita bread is made; a mosaic "rug" in the Deli and mosaic tiles used in a variety of non-traditional ways. Through a window shoppers can watch a mechanical conveyor belt that leads from the pita bread oven. The focal point in the casual dining room is a mosaic clad fountain under a faux sky and the area is enveloped with Mediterranean lifestyle murals. Striped canvas awnings over the openings between "rooms" add a bazaar-like ambiance and small structural columns are covered with mosaic tiles and silver leafed Corinthian caps.

New Yasmeen Bakery is a must-see, must try and buy stop for Mediterranean food gourmets when in Dearborn.

DESIGNER • Marco Design Group, Northville, MI

DESIGN TEAM • Nicholas Gianmarco &
    Kimbery Opipari
    Julie Dugas

GRAPHICS • Kim Opipari & Yashan Young:
    Finishes

FIXTURES & CASES • Kason/H&L Custom
    Cabinetry

REFRIGERATED CASES • Hussmann, Livonia, MI

MURALS • Patri O'Connor, Farmington Hills, MI

WALL FINISHES • BrickTech/Dal Tile/Safran
    Wall Cove

FLOORING • Virginia Tile

LIGHTING • Juno/Abolite/Scavo/Mark Lighting

PHOTOGRAPHY • Laszlo Regos Photography,
    Berkley, MI

EATZI'S
Dallas, TX

What was considered "the hot concept of the year" only a few years ago has, in its way changed people's thinking about what markets are all about. Eatzi's is all about gourmet and specialty foods—prepared and just begging to-go—to be taken home. It is about "Food for the Taking"!

The concept developed by Philip Romano, a successful food marketing impressario and restauranteur, is based on the ever growing popularity of Home Meal Replacement (HMR) in the food industry. People are in a hurry, often both parents or

adults are working, there is less and less desire to cook or prepare meals and yet, at the same time, there is the desire for more interesting, more exciting, palate-tempting foods to dine on. The solution began with partially prepared everyday staple meals that with the advent of Eatzi's and many others in this book has now become an unending selection of fine, freshly prepared gourmet dishes ready to be turned out on the diner's own plates with maybe a quick detour to the microwave oven for a heating.

Eatzi's are now located in Atlanta, Chicago, Washington, San Francisco, Denver, Phoenix and other major cities. The prototype shown here and is the Dallas store, is by TSL/Merchant Design Group of Los Angeles. Tak Toda, president of the design firm said, "The floor plan was the result of careful study and a specific strategy of traffic flow. There are inner and outer loop aisles and traffic travels through the store in a counter clock-wise direction passing around both loops with the Chef's Case presentation as the center point. The customer is exposed to everything in the store in the process." As a focal point of the store's design the Chef's Case not only presents a fabulous array of beautifully prepared and presented entrees and salads but has wines, cradled in their wood cases, lined up in front as well as baskets of freshly baked rolls atop the glass and stainless steel sneeze-guard as "reminders" of what goes with what. Fresh flowers and the bright, light tile lines kitchen/prep area beyond add to the show.

In addition there is the floor-to-ceiling cascade of fresh produce in the Green Market as well as a Field of Green's hand tossed salad bar. In

the Patisserie & Grill items can be purchased "as is" or "custom cooked." The cheese area is an explosion of imported and domestic cheeses while the Charcuterie display entices and excites with a profuse selection of specialty foods. In addition there are a plethora of sauces, condiments, gourmet blended coffees and teas—all available in stores that are usually about 12,000 sq. ft. in size. Why cook when Eatzi's done it all and done it so well?

DESIGNER ◆ TSL Design Group, Los Angeles, CA
OWNER & CREATIVE DIRECTOR OF EATZI'S ◆ Phil Romano & Brinker, Intl.
COLOR CONSULTANTS ◆ Andy Ramsgard, Skaneatles, NY
LOGO DESIGNER & GRAPHICS ◆ Creative Advantage, Little Rock, AK
REFRIGERATED CASES ◆ Hussmann Corp., Chino, CA
STAINLESS STEEL ◆ Watson, Dallas, TX
WALL TILES ◆ Country Floors, Los Angeles, CA
TABLE TILES ◆ Dal Tile, Dallas, TX
PLASTIC LAMINATE ◆ Nevamar, Odenton, MD
LIGHT FIXTURES ◆ Meletio Electric, Dallas, TX
PHOTOGRAPHY ◆ Courtesy of TSL Design Group

HYDE PARK GOURMET FOOD & WINE
Cincinnati, OH

The 2000 sq.ft. Hyde Park Gourmet Food & Wine shop in an historic area of Cincinnati is a browser's delight especially if the browser has an eye for beauty and a taste for the gourmet. As one enters the long and narrow shop designed by the co-owners, Evelyn Ignatow and Sylvia Levine, assisted by Quality Restaurant Supply, one is inundated, enveloped and surrounded by sights and smells and products arranged to attract and ensnare the shopper.

To overcome the feeling of the long space, it has been divided into smaller shopping areas with a lavish display of crusty breads, cheeses and a prep station where deli-delights sandwiches are built to order. Evelyn Ignatow says, "We have a small selection but very high

ARCHITECTURE ◆ Quality Restaurant Supply: Fred Orringer

PROJECT DESIGN TEAM ◆ Eileen Derrick: Perry & Derrick Decorating Center

MILLWORK & CABINETRY ◆ John's Custom Cabinetry

SHELVING/WALL SYSTEMS ◆ Metric and John's Custom Cabinetry

LIGHTING CONSULTANT ◆ Richards Electric

GRAPHICS/SIGNAGE & SPECIAL FINISHES ◆ Greg Courtney

PHOTOGRAPHY ◆ Donald Ventry

end. Our customers tend to be very well traveled and that makes a difference," when it comes to expecting specialty meats and other gourmet items. At the far end of the shop is a fine assortment of domestic and international wines. An oriental style rug laid on the floor plus the weathered timber applied to the walls, the ceiling beams and the old light fixture all create a special ambiance for this shop-within-the-shop.

Along the way to the wine shop one can enjoy gift basket presentations (Ms. Levine's speciality), the Coffee Staytion, or the Food Prep

station where the gourmet carry-out specialties are prepared by Evelyn Ignatow. The two owners are sisters and not only share their love for fine foods and wines but also bring their individual strengths into the mix. Ignatow, besides being the chef, is also in charge of the wine selections, while Levine prepares the gift baskets and also focuses on food items, merchandising and customer service.

In keeping with the historic building which is over 100 years old, the designers used warm, neutral and earth-rich colors such as beige, bisquit and terra cotta along

with both light and dark stained woods. The light colored floor and walls tend to "open" the space and the diagonally laid floor tiles seem to optically expand the space. Industrial style, silvery shelving units contrast with the dark stained woods adjacent to them and the woven wicker and raffia baskets all add to the homey feeling of the store. The casual and friendly hand-written sign cards also contribute to the gracious and welcoming ambiance. Together these things contribute to the very personal and individual attitude of Hyde Park Gourmet.

The Cincinnati papers and trade magazines have "discovered" this personalized Gourmet/Specialty food store and have extolled its virtues.

AMERICAN STORE
Salt Lake City, UT

Step back into the future! Entering the American Store in Salt Lake City is like stepping back into a time warp and finding yourself in some typical American city as it might have looked at the start of the twentieth century. Amidst period shops, street signs, and artifacts of a bye-gone era are some of the newest, upscale, gourmet treats available for today's discriminating and affluent shoppers presented with style—and humor.

Brent Agnew, formerly with American Store Properties and now with Kuey Agnew Design in Park City, UT with the assistance of King Design International, created this warm, friendly and inviting Main St. Marketplace filled with small specialty shops. The newest and finest state-of-the-art equipment and modern conveniences have been integrated into this memory of long ago and patinaed with loving care and excellent display techniques.

The ceiling is painted black and the lights play up the textured shop fronts veneered in old brick and

INTERIOR ARCHITECTURE ◆ Brent Agnew, Kuey Agnew Design, Park City, UT

INTERIOR DESIGN ◆ Brent Agnew and John Bennett

SIGNAGE ◆ King Design International, Eugene, OR

FOR KING DESIGN ◆ Nancy Wade: Design Consultant
Christopher Studack: Design Director

GENERAL CONTRACTOR ◆ HOWA Construction, Salt Lake City, UT

REFRIGERATED CASES ◆ Hussmann, Salt Lake City, UT

PROPS ◆ Brent Agnew, John Bennett, King Design, Int'l.

PHOTOGRAPHY ◆ Courtesy of Brent Agnew

accented with period style signs. The floors change with the departments. Concrete, embedded with leaves, is laid in the Produce area while stained and "worn" wood flooring bedecks the Fish Market. Shoppers stroll down the red brick paved aisles and step off onto wood, vinyl or tile laid floors. The Salty Dog's Seafood shop is capped with a mural painted beneath its brick fascia and the stainless steel refrigerated display case is encased with wood strips. The floor units adjacent to the case are also of the same natural reddish wood. The prep area, behind, is tiled with squares of soft green and cream.

The Deli/Meat area's sign is made of corrugated metal and a metal canopy is supported off it. Here, too, the brick is complemented by the natural woods around the showcases and the amusing wood pushcarts with green canvas canopies that carry the featured products and samples out in the aisles. In addition, there is the Garage, the old-fashioned Pharmacy and even an Ice Cream Shoppe for special treats. Il Sansovino To Go is another unique shop-within-the-shop that features classic Italian foods prepared-to-go or to be eaten within the market in a provided sit down area.

Signage and props are all true to the period from the metal corru-

gated meat market sign, the neon ice-cream cone, the gas station sign hanging next to the roll down garage door of the garage that actually houses a vintage auto—to the crates, bushels, pushcarts, vintage posters and artifacts of a century ago. "All add additional detail to a very interesting market to shop." The store may be small by supermarket standards but it delivers big on product and as an adventure in Gourmet/Speciality food shopping.

ANDRONICO'S MARKET
Iron Horse Plaza, Danville, CA

This upscale market, located in Danville, CA, is the latest adventure in shopping experiences created for Andronico's clientele. According to Bill Andronico, this 41,000 sq.ft. space (including the mezzanine) was designed by Sutti Associates of Burlington, CA to "assault the senses." At once the shoppers start "to interact with our merchandise and our people to get into the whole market experience."

Shoppers are treated to sounds, sights and smells throughout this Mediterranean-inspired interior. Pale green dominates on the tiled walls and on the ceiling. It is complemented by the rich terra cotta tiles and accents as well as many different wood tone finished cases and counters. Blue and ocher tiles are used to accentuate some of the

natural cases with designer specified finishes. The store's color and material palette reinforces the feeling of a garden theme brought indoors with its subtle mixture of colors, woods, rustic furniture, antiques and accessories. Bird houses, garden furniture, hutches and armoires along with silk foliage and the sounds of birds and crickets enhance the ambiance. Contrasting with the rustic textures are the galvanized ceilings that distinguish the Deli and Produce areas as well as the glittering accents of copper, stainless steel, and glass.

"There are trends and then there are lifestyles. Our additions (in the new store) reflect the evolving needs, wants and cravings of the modern shopper," says Bill Andronico whose grandfather, a

DESIGNER/ARCHITECT ◆ Sutti Associates, Burlingame, CA
PRINCIPAL ◆ John Sutti.
ARCHITECT ◆ Jae Lee
INTERIOR DESIGN ◆ Steve Olsen
CONSTRUCTION MANAGER ◆ Steve Berringer
ANDRONICO'S IN-HOUSE MERCHANDISING TEAM ◆ Joyce Mallonee/Laura Stetson/David Guavara
MILLWORK/CABINETRY ◆ Lloyd Gordon Manufacturing, Richmond, CA/GMP Service, Inc., Tracy, CA
SPECIALTY FIXTURES ◆ Magnolia River Mfg., Greeley, CO
REFRIGERATED CASES/COUNTERS ◆ Hussmann, Chino, CA
SHELVING SYSTEMS ◆ Metro
ROTISSERIES/OVENS/KITCHEN DESIGN ◆ Kosmos Assoc., Oakland, CA
GRAPHICS/SIGNAGE ◆ Sutti Assoc. and Baronian Mfg., Concord, CA
SPECIAL FINISHES/MURALS ◆ The Beardley Co., Oakland, CA
AUDIO/VISUAL EQUIPMENT ◆ DMX
PHOTOGRAPHY ◆ Courtesy of Hussmann

Greek immigrant, started this company 80 years ago. Andronico's is like a collection of boutiques gathered in one convenient location and here the discerning and demanding shopper will find fresh produce, the best selection of blended coffees, cheeses, olives and so many other specialties. One of the new additions is the Forno di Andronico which is

the in-store bakery that turns out baguettes, focacia, pizzas, paninis and pastries. The breads are made from organic flour, sea salt and fresh yeast. From a blue and ocher tile trimmed counter in front of the bakery, freshly baked pizzas and panini are available. Nearby is an espresso bar with estate grown coffees stored in giant, ocher colored crocks imported from Germany.

One of the highlights of shopping the Danville Andronico's is the Wine department stocked with over 2500 selections displayed on cedar case shelving. The area features a walk-in, temperature controlled room for premium wines. Three wine stewards are available to assist shoppers in making their selections.

Throughout, the store is filled with beautifully presented foods-to-go. There are entrees-to-go prepared by professional chefs as well as the New Noodle Bar with its many

Asian specialties. Behind a 45 foot long, "L" shaped service case is the store's kitchen with prep stations and equipment in full view of the shoppers. Not only is it an on-going show but shoppers are invited to "taste the wares." As Bill Andronico says, "Anybody who attempts to out a stronger gross by eliminating sampling is a fool." The full service Meat counter boasts of a large variety of sausages as well as Angus beef steaks and Butcher's Choice specializes in marinated meats for the hurried home "chef." The Fish counter overflows with displays of fresh daily catches, shellfish, live lobsters and ready-to-go crab cakes and tuna and salmon patties. Two dozen or more kinds of olives are massed in natural crocks along with capers and assorted antipasti items atop a rich, red toned cabinet with a black granite top. The angled sneeze guard welcomes rather than deters shoppers.

The Nutrition & Health Center is a store within the store with its colorful awnings over the shelves filled with vitamins, food supplements, books and assorted printouts. A full time nutritionist/manager is there to answer special questions. Andronico's has "a large scale and scope but paramount to that, it gives customers a very pleasant shopping experience. Rustic wood finishes in the Bakery and mouth watering smells of baking bread, warm lighting and beautiful produce—all your senses will be delighted."

BRANNON'S MARKET
Little Rock, AK

"The idea was not to bring San Francisco or New York or Paris to Little Rock, but to take the best of what I have seen around the world and build something that would reflect the lifestyle and architecture of our region. It does have a European feel, especially in the Café, but the overall feel is influenced more by Little Rock than anyplace else," says Bran McCarty, the owner and creative force behind Brannon's Market in Little Rock, AK.

Working closely with the talented designers of Marco Design Group of Northville, MI, the 10,000 sq.ft. market combines the usual and traditional fare with the gourmet

DESIGN ◆ Marco Design Group, Northville, MI
PROJECT TEAM ◆ Nicholas Gianmarco/Julie Dugas/Kim Opipari
CONTRACTOR ◆ May Construction Co.
REFRIGERATED CASES/COOLERS ◆ Hussmann Equipment
TABLES & CHAIRS ◆ Pioneer Distributing
SPECIAL FINISHES/MURALS ◆ Mind's Eye Studio, Reggie Adams
LIGHTING ◆ Juno Lighting/Avalanche Ranch/Scott Lamp/PMC Lighting
PHOTOGRAPHY ◆ Laszlo Regos Photography, Berkley, MI

and exotic: hamburgers and tuna fish to quail, pheasant, imported olives and olive oil. "Of course, we carry the staples but also a lot of things you don't expect to find. We want everyone who shops here to find things they need, to find things they didn't know they could get." An in-house chef supervises the kitchen ensuring a flow of gourmet style hot and cold entrees to go or to be enjoyed in the colorful, in-store café.

With the store's compact size, overhead signage seems unnecessary. One has only to follow the scent of freshly baked breads or brewed coffee—or the aroma of flowers flown in several times a week. The layout complements the hurried shopper's lifestyle as well as that of the more leisurely shopper who takes time to enjoy the attractive displays along the way and finds unexpected treasures as well. The flooring is concrete treated in assorted earth tone colors to create an overall terra cotta finish. This is complemented by the wood beams that over the high ceiling. Earthy ocher colors, accented with terra cotta, are used on the walls and there are also accent portions of "stone-work" as well as faux finished columns enhanced with amusing paintings. The same light touch is evident in the cut-out "mural" of cows that graces the fascia in the dairy area. Laminates resembling wood, marble, stone and other textures are used throughout.

Shoppers may enter near the check-out counters or through the more aromatic one that leads to the bakery and coffee areas and the burst of color that attracts one to the Produce department.. Just ahead are the Prepared Foods and Deli counters and the brightly colored tables and chairs of the Café in the Produce area. The key points in the store are the Village Greens (Produce), Dahleng's Meat Co., McGillis Fish Co., and La Charcuterie (cheeses, olives, smoked fish and cold cuts). These are clus-

tered together. In addition, rows of gondolas are grouped in the central area for canned goods and staples. Frozen Foods and Dairy are located along one long perimeter wall.

"This store is a work in progress," says McCarty. "We have a lot of specialty items and it takes time to see whether or not they will sell. But in prepared and baked foods we already know that people want more of what we have and want a greater variety." "People are looking for convenience, a store where they can find what they want and get in and out quickly. But they're also looking for a place that carries items they may have seen around the country and now know they can find in Little Rock. It's like having a neighborhood market that is worldly in scope."

BRISTOL FARMS
Mission Viejo, CA

There is no specific corporate look that defines Bristol Farms. Each of the present eight units is designed as a typical specialty food store targeted at a particular market. There is the look of the neighborhood designed into each unit and if there is a theme the theme is "This is where we are at."

Deborah English, formerly VP of Store Development for Bristol Farms and now the principal of RED Studio, Long Beach, CA has designed most of the units in this chain and does use certain design elements and materials in common. "We use a lot of hand painted murals and constructed architectural theming such as facades. We have the people who make movie sets build these facades for us." For the 26,750 sq.ft. Bristol Farms built in Mission Viejo, the designer's concept is targeted at affluent, educated shoppers who appreciate a market that specializes in gourmet prepared foods and imported specialities. Deborah English creates an emotional connection between the store and the community. There is a unique interpretation of the architectural treasures

of the nearby San Juan Capistrano Mission interlaced with the exposed, modern structure with its large concrete beams and contemporary lighting scheme. Daylight—or the sense of daylight—is important to these shoppers who do enjoy an out-of-doors lifestyle. To create that "daylight" feeling the ceiling has been pushed up to 22 feet and light blue/gray tiles cover it. The walls are finished in light and bright colors and the up-lighting enhances the daylight ambiance. A large, Diego Rivera style sun dominates the space from its location over the produce area. From most areas in the store the warmth and brilliance of the sun can be seen and felt.

Porcelain tile floors are used in this installation as they are in other Bristol Farm units as are the large, hand painted murals that wrap around the fresh produce area. Faux palenta plaster and stone finishes abound and add texture as well as refer to the Old Mission structure. The Fine Meats department and the Prepared Foods service line near the

DESIGN ◆ RED Studio, Long Beach, CA; Deborah English & Lisa Johnson

ARCHITECT ◆ Musil Govan Azzalino, Irvine, CA; Dan Cline

CONTRACTOR ◆ Savant Construction, Downey, CA

FIXTURES ◆ Killion Enterprises, Vista CA/JF Fixtures, Long Beach, CA/Hare Enterprises, Long Beach, CA/Newood Display Manufacturing Co., Eugene, OR

REFRIGERATED CASES ◆ Hussmann, Bridgeton, MO

FURNITURE ◆ Fine Wood Finish, Huntington Beach, CA/JF Fixtures, Long Beach, CA/Oasis, Malibu, CA/Newood Display Fixture Mfg. Co., Eugene, OR

SIGNAGE & GRAPHICS ◆ Maximum Visibility, Topango, CA

MURALS ◆ Stewart Magee Murals, Pomona, CA

THEMING ◆ Lexington Scenery & Props, Sun Valley, CA

FAUX FINISHES ◆ Bennett & Thomas, Laguna Beach, CA

Café seem to be the ground floor levels of old stone buildings while the fascia of the dairy area is pierced with stone framed "windows" in the adobe textured surface. Overhanging the building is a native, red tiled roof supported by dark, weathered

wood corbels. The dark wood takes over in Produce where the "farm stands" gather out on the floor to showcase the fruits and vegetables. Wrought iron, also part of the Mission style heritage, naturally graces the Wine and Spirits area and the check-out counters. In the Wine area, wrought iron arches float over the stained wood floor units and overhead in checkout the decorative

gates serve to support the pendant light fixtures that highlight and light up this zone. "This is the first time I've used iron work," says Ms. English but she found that these lacy light units not only added to the desired Mission ambiance effectively contained the necessary lighting

Atop the Coffee area is a hand carved foam frieze made to simulate stone. "Carved" onto the band are words like "harvest," "grain," "reap," and "sow." Says Deborah English, "They are a collection of life-giving words about growing and eating." These words invoke images of freshness and life and that is what Bristol Farms is about.

BYERLY'S
Maple Grove, MN

Lund Food Holdings is a family owned chain of upscale markets and the family's traditions and values trace back to three generations. Under the company's new president and CEO, Russell T. Lund, lll, grandson of the founder, the firm has expanded and now includes the new Byerly's in Maple Grove, MN. This Byerly's, part of the takeover of the upscale chain by Lund, features a "mainstreet design that establishes a 'downtown' feel for the community." Robert M. Gorski, the designer, says,"Byerly's unique architecture blends a large store format into a small pedestrian- friendly center." The 57,000 sq.ft. store is also the first that demonstrates how "a high fashion ambiance can be adapted to a full service supermarket." When it comes to food display and presentation, John Pazahanik, VP of Lund's Store Development, said, "We recognized (with this new store) a prime oppportunity to introduce an identifiable brand personality for the chain. We looked at every aspect for a new overall decor—finishes-the color palette—fixturing, and of course, lighting."

After researching the best of retailing in the up market Twin Cities area Robert Gorski came to the conclusion that "creating zones of high contrast lighting encourages consumer purchasing." "Our challenge was to economically translate this into a consistent, value-added theme." Byerly's Maple Grove store was based on "applying the building blocks of modern supermarket; including lighting, signage, and visual merchandising." In designing the lighting plan, Gorski used only one resource for lamps and one for the lighting fixtures yet still created special lighting effects for each area in the store.

In the Bakery and Artisan Bread shops, the reddish stained wood complements the freshly baked products while the textured, woven baskets used to hold the breadstuff add a homey and hearty quality to the foods. The Produce department is distinguished by a three foot clerestory that reaches up to the 16 foot ceiling. This glowing crown of pseudo windows is illuminated by 32 watt T8 3000K fluorescent lamps. The milk white diffuser panels are screened with a pattern resembling real wire glass.

To emphasize its location, the designer created an angled dropped ceiling and corresponding crown fascia over the Deli area. The movement of the ceiling echoes the angular turns of the counter below which is further accentuated by a band of deep reddish wood and by the pattern of light beige tiles separated from the darker tiles by a terra cotta band Here, the illumination combines fluorescents with spots plus internally illuminated cases. The Meat and Seafood shops are lined up along the perimeter wall with a wide soffit above and light streams down from behind the broad beige band. Gorski used a wood trellis motif in several

INTERIOR DESIGN ◆ RMG Design, Eden Prairie, MN; Robert M. Gorski

ARCHITECT ◆ KKE Architects, Inc. Minneapolis, MN

STORE PLANNING/LAYOUT ◆ Design Services Group

LIGHTING DESIGN ◆ Robert M. Gorski

GENERAL CONTRACTOR ◆ Opus Corp., Northwest, MN

MILLWORK/CABINETRY ◆ Capitol Wood Products,/Premier Restaurant Equipment

FIXTURES/CASES ◆ Kasson/Barker

REFRIGERATED CASES ◆ Tyler

SHELVING/WALL SYSTEM ◆ Lozier

GRAPHICS/SIGNAGE ◆ Signergy

Throughout the store the color palette is soft, warm and neutral. Assorted beiges and cream colors are used on everything from the carpeted and tiled floors to the metal and laminate facings on the cases to the walls that were faux painted Mission Style to create a variety of textures. Light natural woods and wood toned laminates are used on the floor cases and counters. The flattering color palette is accented with a rich, earthy terra cotta, and all the colors respond to the selected lamps to give off a warm, upscale and truly elegant setting for the food shopping experience.

When you see the Living Wise symbol, you know products in this area are...

areas within the market. In the Living Wise department, located in a rear corner next to the Produce and Dairy areas, a wood trellis was suspended 11 feet off the floor and the ceiling above was painted out to achieve a sense of intimacy. Low voltage, 75 watt MR16s are integrated into the trellis and the track fixtures form a plastic pattern overhead. The trellis was repeated, in a larger scale, in Bachman's Flower Shop.

In the elegant Wine & Spirits shop there is a lavish display of bottles on crates out on the floor as well as in the wood wall cubicles. This

area is illuminated by MR16s mounted on ceiling tracks. The Café has a seating area for the convenience and comfort of shoppers. In a residential setting with a wide expanse of windows and a welcoming fireplace, shoppers can take a break from their shopping and indulge in some of the Byerly's specialties presented in glass enclosed cases out front of the café.

Based on the effectiveness of the design of this store, seven other Byerly's in the chain are being remodeled based on the successful prototype.

ZAGARA'S
Jenkintown, PA

Situated on the ground floor level of what was once a Wanakaker's Department store is the newest and most exciting of the Zagara's Markets. The Zagara name—Italian for orange blossom—is well known in the New Jersey and Pennsylvania area as an outstanding provider of specialty and natural foods. In a landmarked 1950's building, the designers/architects of Shook Design Group of Charlotte, NC, using scintillating art deco motifs, created a shopping experience especially targeted at the "time-poor" but affluent and educated consumers of this area.

The art deco concept, according to Kevin Kelley, principal in charge of the design team, came from John Zagara, the founder of the company. "Art deco celebrated a time when people had money and it captures a mood and a spirit of the roaring twenties when people really celebrated a lot," says Kelley, but even more it complements the straight and sharp lines of the building's architecture. The sophisticated design approach, according to Kelley, appeals to the " busy, health-conscious but epicurean food adventurer."

The interior is divided into a series of shops that seem to flow from one into the next. Zig-zag lines predominate on the floor in intricate art deco patterns of vinyl tiles. These angles are complemented by the white stepped soffit overhead that also moves sharply back and forth and sometimes sweeps out in a soft, swelling curve. In the Body Natural area the floor is concrete to provide a more " earthy" or "natural" feeling to the space. The zig-zag motif also helps to reinforce the "Z" in Zagara. On the sharp in and out turns of the aforementioned soffit, the shops are

identified by the peg mounted letters applied to the frieze.

Because of the state of the building's construction, the designers had to camouflage many of the "service" elements such as the electrical con-

duits, refrigeration piping and the pipes and ducts of the HVAC system. Since there are other tenants in the building and the architects couldn't go above or below slab, it became the designer's task to organize

and hide what they could. Some of the giant columns, painted the same color as the soffit, are decorated with a multitude of brightly colored pipes—disguising their true purpose. Passing from the Bakery, Deli and Prepared Foods areas into the Meat, Poultry, and Seafood shops, the shopper passes under a striking and dominant sunburst design. The eight foot arch below the sunburst actually conceals a six foot section of duct. Another example of camouflaging the pipes and ducts.

According to John Zagara, "What we wanted to do was, in a sense, subconsciously convey the image of each department as a separate, family- owned entity." The sweeping soffits over some of the shops help to identify and separate them as do the different colored tiles on the back walls of these departments. The blue and green tiles in Seafood suggest water while the white tiles in the

DESIGN ◆ Shook Design Group, Charlotte, NC

DESIGN TEAM ◆ Kevin Kelley, AIA; Principal in charge

Mike Nicholls, AIA: Project Architect

Kevin O'Donnell: V.M. Director

Cecily Worrell: Interior Designer Colleen Duffy & Stan Rostas, AIA

ARCHITECT ◆ McGillin Architects, Inc. Bala Cynwood, PA

IN-HOUSE DESIGN TEAM ◆ Zagara's Specialty & Natural Foods, Mt. Laurel, NJ

John Zagara: Owner

Kevin Sheffield: Store Designer

Lou Anselmi: Project Manager

FIXTURES ◆ Borgen Systems, Des Moinres, IA/Hussmann, Bridgeton, MO/Barker Co., Keosaugua, IA

FURNITURE ◆ GAR, Lakewood, NJ/Home on the Range, Durham, NC

GRAPHICS ◆ Sign-A-Rama, Willow Grove, PA

LIGHTING ◆ Donovan, Brooktondale,NY/FLOS, Huntington Sta., NY/Juno, Norcross, GA./Koch & Lowy, Avon, MA/Ron Rezek, New York, NY

PHOTOGRAPHY ◆ Tim Buchman

Meat section was used to make the space appear "clean and sterile." In addition, there are giant murals in the Seafood and Produce areas. The mural in Produce is angled forward off the wall to give "a sense of entry" to the space and further the sense of discovery that Zagara wanted his customers to feel in the store.

Most of the exposed casework in stainless steel. Kevin O'Donnell of the Shook Design team says that the polished finish not only says "clean" but it implies "gourmet." In the Café Z the cases are finished in red and green laminates. Baskets, bushels, trellises and other softening props have been added to create the desired warm and inviting ambiance.

Kevin Kelley says, "We equated food with fashion. It's fashionable to learn about food and how to assemble it." Zagara's Market is a fashionable excursion into Specialty and Natural food presentation. By the use of line, color, texture and light—and a sense of theater—Shook Design Group, working with John Zagara, created a truly pleasurable fashion/shopping experience.

GELSON'S MARKET
West Hollywood, CA

Though the 18,000 sq. ft. Gelson's Market in West Hollywood is the smallest market in this upscale chain of food stores, it is "larger than life" in its design and appeal to its particular clientele. According to Nancy Wade of King Design International, the designers of this store, "When we were asked to design for Gelson's West Hollywood, we knew that this store would have to be extraordinary to appeal to the community—a sophisticated clientele accustomed to everyday surroundings that are often 'larger than life.'" Taking their cues from the movies and the "land

of make believe," the design team created "illusions" in the best theatrical sense. "Actually, sometimes art really does imitate life, as we proved with the installation of dramatic faux brownstone on many of the store's walls. Add to the dramatic 'stone' walls the contemporary beauty of colorful sunburst murals that splash over onto some adjacent walls and aisle markers and you begin to define the flavor of this decor."

The store itself, a big box Mayfair Market that was taken over by Gelson's, was redone by MCG Architecture of Pasadena and King Design International of Eugene, OR. Robert Stiles, the president of Gelson's knew what he wanted and he got what he hoped for. Considering that the usual Gelson store runs between 26,000 sq.ft. and 32,000 sq. ft., it took creative planning and paring down to add some of the shops-within-the-shop that his particular

DESIGN ◆ Interior: King Design International,
   Eugene, OR
   Becky Phegley: Design Consultant
   Christopher Studach: Design Director
   Martin Wernick: Designer
ARCHITECT ◆ MCG Architecture, Pasadena, CA
GENERAL CONTRACTOR ◆ A.J. Padelford, Los
   Angeles, CA
REFRIGERATION CASES ◆ Edison Source,
   Anaheim, CA
PROPS & DECORATIVES ◆ Pam Smith, Gelson's,
   Encino, CA
PHOTOGRAPHY ◆ Longs Photography, Los
   Angeles, CA

clientele would expect. A Bakery/ Coffee shop was added in a small, carved out niche and a Floral department was added in the front of the store which was bumped out four feet to accommodate it. Produce became a corner shop and since a real skylight was structurally unfeasible, a bright sun motif appears and reappears throughout the store and fluffy styrofoam clouds float in a patch of blue sky over the Bakery. Pam Smith, of Gelson's, provided many amusing and unique artifacts and decorative props that also enliven the space. Wrought iron accessories and faux greenery enhance the settings. Colorful murals appear on the walls in Fresh Meats and Delicatessen areas while double faced, flat decorative graphics dangle along the perimeter walls. Warm and cool colored Amtico flooring is used in the Bakery Coffee Shop as well as

in the handsome, self contained Wine & Spirits shop.

Throughout, three dimensional "stone" walls and imaginative concepts were used to add to the illusion such as the white painted window frames filler with clear and stained glass. Says Nancy Wade, "Certainly, nobody would suspect the presence of the styrofoam that lurks just beneath a painted surface." "Much like the legendary movie sets typical of this town, the walls create an illusion of grandeur that is not easily disproved."

Gelson's Market has not only kept the former shoppers but has attracted a whole new breed of specialty store shoppers. According to Becky Phegley, the Design Consultant on this project, West Hollywood is full of film people, "artsy" types and it has a sizable "gay" population—all of whom

would appreciate the light touch that distinguishes this Gelson's. As Nancy Wade sums it up, "It's dramatic! It's colorful! It's beautiful! It's larger than life!"

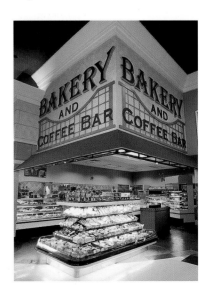

FOOD EMPORIUM
Bridge Market, New York, NY

Combine great architectural details, a romantic location with a breath-taking view, and top class presentation of specialty foods arranged like living masterpieces and what do you have? It is the new Food Emporium Bridge Market located under the Queensborough or 59th St. Bridge in New York City. The Emporium is only one part of the 98,000 sq. ft. Bridge Market complex envisioned and brought to glorious reality by Sir Terence Conran working with the architectural firm of Hardy Holzman Pfeiffer Associates of New York. Already blossoming in the complex is a Conran Home Furnishing store and a super elegant gourmet restaurant, Guastavino's.

The architecture is what one first sees in the Food Emporium. There is the profusion of multi-paned windows with arched tops securely located between the multi-faceted, tile covered piers and then there are

the fabulous sweeps of vaulted ceilings that reach up to a spectacular height of 40 feet. The walls, columns and arched ceilings are all covered in 6" x 12" ceramic tiles intricately arranged in basketweave and herringbone patterns. Food Emporium, a subsidiary of the A&P Company covers 35,000 sq. ft. of which over 16,000 sq. ft. is devoted to selling space. This is larger than the usual Food Emporium store and it has become the chain's flagship.

Sam Burman, A&P's VP of Store Planning & Design was faced with many problems because of the landmark status of the site. Nothing could be suspended or attached to the soaring ceilings so Burman had to develop special floor units and gondolas which would allow the ductwork to run through alongside the gondola shelves. Other ductwork floats in a soffit that runs between the prep area and the vault.

The floor units all had to contain their own built-in lighting. "There is no ambient lighting," says Burman. "By using the built-in lighting there are no shadows and the foods are glorified by most T5's and metal halides." With the wonderful windows, the vast amount of daylight available and the view beyond, Burman had to "maintain the transparency of the walls to allow uninterrupted views into the interior's cathedral-like space." "The windows all have electrical blinds with sun sensors that will cause them to go up or down automatically: these blinds are semi-translucent." Fixtures and/or shelving units that would ordinarily be set along the perimeter walls now are part of an even more open plan. The fascinating prep area is now on view from outside and a sheer glass wall separates the grocery area from its upscale restaurant neighbor.

Imported Italian gray and beige porcelain tiles with abrasive surfaces are used on the floors. They were selected to go with the existing "historical" ceiling tiles. For the interior walls, Canadian gray granite, polished to a smooth sheen, was used and imported painted glass and mosaic tiles were used throughout as decorative accents. Roger Turley, VP of Food Emporium, remarked that

"These distinctive mosaics—unique to each market shop—identifies the areas and reduces the need for signage in the store." Cherry wood and stainless steel completed the materials palette and they were used for the floor fixtures and the back bar areas.

Burman describes shopping this Food Emporium as visiting an "open market" for Produce and Flowers

DESIGNER DESIGN TEAM ◆ A&P Co., Montvale, NJ
Sam Burman: VP Store Planning & Design
Jose Pimentel: Manager of Design
Bert Fontanilla: Senior Designer Planning
& Design
CONTRACT DESIGN ◆ Rosenbaum Design
Group, New York, NY
Roy Rosenbaum: Principal
Frank Yulo: Associate
Paul Fahey: Staff Architect
ARCHITECT ◆ Hardy Holzman Pfeiffer
Associates, New York, NY
GRAPHICS/GLASS/MOSAIC/FIXTURES ◆ Roland
Gebhardt Design, New York, NY
FIXTURES/FURNITURE ◆ Bergen Sales (BSI),
Butler, NJ/MEI, Chicago, IL
GLASS & MOSAICS ◆ Franz Mayer of Munich,
New York, NY
FLOORING ◆ Azrock, Florence, AL/Pro-Tile
Distributors, New York, NY
GRAPHICS & SIGNAGE ◆ Ruitenberg Display,
Paterson, NJ. SPI, Brantford, ON
LIGHTING DESIGN ◆ Lightron, Cornwall,
NY/Mark Lighting, Edison, NJ
MILLWORK ◆ Paramount Fixture Sales Co.,
Nrewark, NJ
PHOTOGRAPHY ◆ Esto, Courtesy of A&P,
Montvale, NJ

and then visiting the shops-within-the-shop for specialty products such as the Seafood Cove with its own Sushi and Clam bar, the Corner Bakery for hand made and freshly baked breads, rolls and pastries and the Place for Meat shop for special cuts. Each shop has a distinct look like the Eight O'Clock Coffee stand which is topped by the brilliant red and yellow oval shaped, oversized bag topper. Here shoppers can not only buy their preferred beans or grinds but indulge in a cup of freshly brewed coffee.

Turley says, "Food Emporium's objective is to create a place where customers can come and congregate, see their neighbors, and pass the time of day." Bridge Market has become an "in spot" and the efforts of the various architects, designers and craftspersons along with the in-store personnel has made this Food Emporium the "must" shopping spot.

KOWALSKI'S
Woodbury, MN

Kowalski's is part of a vision—a part of a grand city scheme. The architecture of the 48,000 sq. ft. big box store features rich brick work and refined details such as the Tudor style slate roofs, the curved glass building corner towers and the fully screened loading docks. "The character truly reflects the upscale marketplace atmosphere as well as blends with the architectural concept established at the City Hall" which is part of the new "downtown" look for Woodbury, MN. Also scheduled for this master plan are a library and an indoor city park.

This is Kowalski's fourth store though it is also the first to be built from the ground up. KKE Architects of Minneapolis, MN was the architectural firm used to create this store and Robert M. Gorski of RMG Designs designed the interior of "the upscale, state-of-the-art grocery." The street level is capped with a

mezzanine over the Produce area. This area is flooded with daylight streaming in from the arched windows that run along that side of the building. The concrete floor is dyed a rich, deep terra cotta color and scored off in a diagonal grid of four foot squares. Wood and black metal stands and crates add to the European open market feeling of the space. The pressed metal ceiling is lowered and finished with a coffered pattern. Halide cans are recessed into the ceiling while additional spots are applied and targeted at the floor product displays.

A village-like ambiance seems to permeate the interior with faux painted walls in earthy ochers, golds, rusts and terra cotta and architectural accents such as moldings, window frames, cornices, roof lines and more. Added to all this are the cherry wood highlights and friezes. The flower shop looks like it might have been lifted up in the Province and deposited here in the store. It has a rusty stucco textured facade, applied clocks and a sculpturally enriched balcony that projects out over the entrance. The gray/green painted window moldings and door frame the well illumi-

nated interior of the mini shop and the abundant floral display. The same Provincial atmosphere carries through to the extensive Gift Shop where country style, rustic farm tables support some of the stock while other products are set out in old library bookcases. Hanging from an old metal gate that is suspended from the ceiling are assorted planters, lanterns and artifacts. Point source lighting dominates most of the store with fluorescent lamps over the gondolas in the grocery area. White Son and Mastercolor lamps by Phillips are used.

The Meat department appears to be located on the ground level of a two story white stucco and brick trimmed house complete with dormer windows. While all appears to be "antique" above eye level, the cases and counters are satin finished, stainless steel and the walls of the prep area are covered with muted, earth toned tiles. The Café is flanked by a row of wide and tall windows, and a stone fireplace makes it feel warm and inviting. It also ties this

space back to the rest of the European village theme.

Services at Kowalski include catering, cooking classes, floral arranging, a salon to pamper the shopper, personalized shopping as well as an e-mail grocery system for placing and picking up orders. "With all the traditional 'downtown' amenities located under one roof, the City of Woodbury has embraced this unique concept and the owner and design team are proud of delivering a totally new concept in grocery history."

INTERIOR DESIGN ◆ RMG Designs, Eden Prairie, MN; Robert M. Gorski
ARCHITECTURE ◆ KKE Architects, Minneapolis, MN
MILLWORK/CABINETRY ◆ Northtown Millwork
SPECIALTY CASES & FIXTURES ◆ Barker
REFRIGERATED CASES ◆ Hussmann
ROTISSERIES/OVENS ◆ Luck's Ovens
SHELVING/WALL SYSTEMS ◆ Lozier
SPECIAL FINISHES/MURALS ◆ Tivoli
PHOTOGRAPHY ◆ Courtesy of KKE Architects

KONMAR MARKET
Leidschendam, Netherlands

The Konmar Markt located in a small town outside of Rotterdam, Leideschendam is a cross between a gourmet specialty shop and a supermarket. Display, merchandise presentation and ambiance is everywhere in the store. The shopper is never aware of the building's envelop because he or she is being led through the criss-crossing aisles, past the well illuminated displays, the costumed chefs, cooks and food handlers always on show, and the bold graphics that also serve as signage.

This new concept store called Formula 2000 was designed for the Konmar group by Michael Peters

Group, BV of Amsterdam. The name not only is based on the millennium year but on the principle that it takes 2000 sq. meters to produce this market. The floor layout is based on adjacencies: products that go with other products are shown next to one another. As seen on the floor plan, the store consists of nine major shops-within-the shop and the perimeter walls carry the assorted groceries, non food products and such. An unusual touch is that the working bakery is located at the far end of the store but it is still "in touch" with the Prepared Foods, the Coffee & Tea shop, and the Fresh Juice and Wine & Beer areas.

Interestingly, wines and beers appear
on many of the food counters as
"accessories" to the prepared foods-
to-go. The "right" wine is shown
with the selected cheeses, with the
meats, seafood, etc. The center of
the store houses the cheese, eggs
and poultry shop. Each "shop" is
actually a four sided, full round unit
with service counters and cases on
three sides and a prep area or
kitchen in the back when required.

The servers, in white chef's
coats, wear color coded bandanas
around their necks and matching
hats or ribbons on straw hats. They

DESIGN • Michael Peters Group, Amsterdam
FIXTURES • Wanzl
PHOTOGRAPHY • John Marshall

are part of the live action show that adds to the spirit and uniqueness of this specialty store. They are knowledgeable and are actually cooks who use their allotted space to prepare the special cuts of meat, slice off a chunk of cheese, scoop up the shellfish or prepare the salads and entrees to-go. As a special courtesy to their shoppers, Konmar has instituted interactive "Recet'O'Maats" or Recipe Stations where shoppers are offered recipes that are right for the time of year, the products and produce that are fresh and available and somewhat different than the usual fare. In addition to showing what the food can look like there are recipes and cooking instructions which can be printed out by the interested shopper. A convenient shopping list is also included—and everything on it is available in the store.

Up front, near the entrance, is the Flower Shop and the check-out counters as well as a well manned Customer Service desk. Service, specialties and a big smile are served up regularly at Konmar along with a diverse selection of native and imported gourmet treats.

SAINSBURY'S
Greenwich Peninsula, London, UK

The new concept store for the chain of Sainsbury supermarkets was built next to the Millennium Dome in Greenwich—just outside of London. The Amalgam Design firm of London created this—"the world's first low-energy supermarket." It was designed to be environmentally friendly and energy efficient as well as introduce the specialist food servery counters.

Customer research found that though Sainsbury scored higher on brand loyalty than any other food retailer in the UK, many customers found them "too formal, too authoritative, and out-of-date." A major part of this new design was geared at changing that image for a more open and customer-friendly one. The "servery counters," as designed here, are "areas for customer communication and are perceived as the highlights of the shopping experience." The servery counters are all cobalt blue and thus are readily recognized throughout the store. All the jewel-like colors used in the store are "specialist food-safe paint finishes" and they were used instead of the more traditional ceramic wall tiles. These allowed the designers a much greater freedom and the ability to use exactly the colors they wanted when and where they were needed.

Specialty foods and gourmet foods are now presented in a

DESIGN ◆ Amalgam, London, UK
DESIGN TEAM ◆ Glyn Hawkins/Margery Craig/Mark Simpson/Chris Hall/Sarah Wenman
ARCHITECT ◆ Chetwoods
SAINSBURY'S DESIGN STAFF ◆ Anthea Nicholson Cole/Damian Culkin
PHOTOGRAPHY ◆ Norman Hollands

warmer and friendlier environment. To make the Bakery/Patisserie more visually accessible, a structural glass wall was placed between the actual bakery and the bread counter up front. This puts the baking activity on show without compromising the efficiency of the real and very busy bakery. "The saturated fruit colors were chosen to emphasize the fine patisseries while the bakery was communicated through large scale photography."

To communicate the sense of a commercial kitchen in the Fish & Meat shop, the prep area was inte-

grated into the servery counter. Prepared orders are placed onto a brightly lit "pass-over" area and then forward atop the counter. Deli customers expect and want to see "a traditional approach with the emphasis on abundance" research showed. To do this Amalgam's designers used cherry wood and aubergine paint "to create a rich, modern interpretation of an Italian Deli." The shoppers' responses have been overwhelmingly favorable. Beech wood and stainless steel are teamed up in the Salad Kitchen up front. The combination of materials creates a modern kitchen look while the vivid green paint "conveys the salad offer."

The light terrazzo flooring, the light filled ceilings and the stainless steel accents throughout the store create a fresh, bright interior for the specialty foods. Red and black directional signs hanging in the open space and the dimensional white letters on the photo blow-ups of products over the perimeter shops make getting around the new store easy and fun.

VICTORY MARKET
Leominster, MA

"The idea was to create a convenient, fast-food format for today's time-poor customers. We wanted to create an open market environment and place all the meal solutions in one location We also wanted to create a pinball effect where our customers could bounce from one area to another rather than be limited to aisles," says Jay DiGeronimo, Jr., the president of Victory Market.

Working closely with Riesenburger, Leenhouts & Associates of Rochester, NY, a design firm which has worked on other Victory projects, the new Market Square format evolved. It was introduced in the 65,000 sq.ft. Leominster, MA free standing store.

Though the design simulates an outdoor market, warmth permeates throughout the space. From the quarry tile floors to the burnt sienna open roof deck, the palette is filled with earthy, warm and neutral colors. Upon entering the store, the Produce area bursts forth in rich color under the carefully selected lamps. Fresh vegetables and fruits

are displayed on natural oak, tilt tables that are on casters. The same natural oak is used to veneer the refrigerated cases. The cases up front are self contained so they can be moved without concerns regarding pipes and drainage.

The "scatter plan" clusters the specialty foods to encourage add-on sales. The meal solution area is located around the Produce zone and the foods are prepared in full view of the shoppers as they move through the space. "We wanted to bring our staff onto the floor and

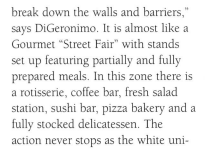

DESIGN ◆ Riesenburger Leenhouts & Associates, Rochester, NY

ARCHITECT ◆ Ed Courmier

MECHANICAL DESIGN ◆ The Darcy Co., Holyoke, MA

TILT TABLES ◆ Kason Market Products, Franklin Park, IL

SELF CONTAINED CASES/FEATURE CASES ◆ Barker Co., Keosaugua, IA

REFRIGERATED CASES ◆ Hill Phoenix, Colonial Heights, VA./Hussmann

WALK-IN COOLER ◆ Tyler Refrigeration, Niles, MI

ROTISSERIES ◆ Hickory Industries, N.Bergen, NJ

MILLWORK/SPECIAL FIXTURES/SHELVING ◆ Kent Corp., Birmingham, AL

LIGHTING & POWER GRID ◆ Amerlux, Fairfield, NJ

PHOTOGRAPHY ◆ Courtesy of Riesenburger Leenhouts & Associates

break down the walls and barriers," says DiGeronimo. It is almost like a Gourmet "Street Fair" with stands set up featuring partially and fully prepared meals. In this zone there is a rotisserie, coffee bar, fresh salad station, sushi bar, pizza bakery and a fully stocked delicatessen. The action never stops as the white uni-formed chefs and cooks at the vari-ous stands are seen preparing the assorted dishes which are then temptingly displayed up front.

Color corrected fluorescent lamps are used in the Produce area and metal halides light up the gen-eral areas. The open ceiling allows greater flexibility in lighting and the designers custom tailored a grid system which has total flexibility for the equipment and the power supply for the fluorescents and HIDs. The success of the Market Square concept—the new look for Victory Markets—is based on the flexibility and adaptability of the whole concept.

LCBO
Byward Market, Ottawa, ON

The Liquor Control Board of Ontario, a state owned and operated wine and liquor retailer, has many freestanding stores throughout the province of Ontario in Canada. In creating this 20,000 sq. ft., two-level store in Byward Market in Ottawa, Fiorino Design of Toronto created a noteworthy flagship store for LCBO. The concept behind the design was to further LCBO's goal of establishing itself as an "entertaining, educational and appealing place to shop" in an area surrounded by embassies, consulates and demanding and knowledgeable clients.

The design reflects two shopping options. The entry level presents the general product line while on the lower level "Vintage"—the fine wines and premium entertainment ideas, which was originally introduced in a prototype design in the Bayview Village store. The more intimate atmosphere of the lower level is more club-like and is reminiscent of a chateau cellar.

The flowing plans invite shoppers to explore and browse. At ground level the oval shaped power aisle is enhanced by feature areas such as the Gift area, the Beer area

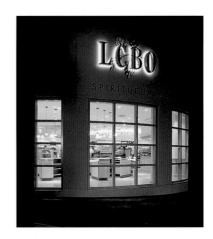

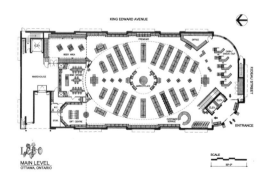

LCBO
MAIN LEVEL
OTTAWA, ONTARIO

SCALE

and the Demonstration Kitchen, while a secondary power aisle cuts across the oval and connects to the Central Market Place. The colors used on this level emphasize "the romantic origin" of the product with an ambiance suggestive of a sunny courtyard. The yellow stuccoed perimeter walls are accented with sage and ivory. A metal chandelier

DESIGN ◆ Fiorino Design Inc., Toronto, ON
   Nella Fiorino
FIXTURE CONTRACTOR ◆ Hutton Bielmann
   Design, Inc., London, ON
GENERAL CONTRACTOR ◆ Westinde
   Construction Ltd., Napean, ON
LIGHTING ◆ Lightolier
DECORATIVE PENDANT LIGHTING ◆ Barbican
   Architectural Products, Ltd.
MURALS ◆ David Adolphus
PLASTIC FINISHES ◆ Nevamar/Formica/Wilsonart
SPECIAL PAINT FINISHES ◆ Moss & Lam
PHOTOGRAPHER ◆ David Whittaker

with rustic glass uplights is poised over the customer service area and it is accented with a hand-painted trompe l'oeil on the ceiling of grapes, vines and hops.

Custom fixture were developed by the designers and they include double sided perimeter fixtures with merchandising and display capabilities and rolling displays and nesting tables that group coordinating beverages and accessories.

The Vintages or lower level shop "engages customers with a higher level of product and ambiance." The circular plan divides the space into focused shopping areas. The curved traffic aisle flows into a series of three arched and vaulted alcoves reminiscent of wine caves and then into a central Rotunda area. A Tasting Room is located at the back end of the space. Honey onyx glass

doors set into pearwood stained maple cabinetry, lime painted tongue and groove beamed ceilings, and the patterned sand and bisque tiling on the floors all are complemented by the paneled walls finished by ocher and the finely troweled stucco walls and domed ceiling. Custom wrought iron work, borrowed from chateau wine cellars, adds to the look and texture of the space. The ironwork appears on door grills, the honey onyx light fixtures and the stairway balustrade, The custom pendant fixtures identify the customer service desk and check-out counters. A

unique custom chandelier over nesting display tables highlights select wine accessories.

Throughout, the designers emphasized the romantic and natural origin of the products and conveyed that concept with "subtle but consistent connections through color, texture, art, and wine, spirit and beer producing agents."

LCBO, MINI STORE
Covent Garden, London, UK

The LCBO Mini-Store is a new concept for the Liquor Control Board of Ontario and this design is also the first store built for LCBO outside of Canada. The 2400 sq. ft. sq. space is in one of the newly opened retail spots in the Covent Garden indoor marketplace in London. LCBO joins with another 49 vendors to offer merchandise in this very "in" place in London. The original market was located here back in 1820 but was demolished and replaced with a new entertainment/shopper/meeting place complex several years ago. This is a new addition to the exciting, friendly and almost always people-jammed space. The LCBO shop also complements the fine selection of International cuisine offered by other vendors in the Covent Garden neighborhood.

Subtle colors and textures were blended to create this "unique, comfortable 'specialty shop' environment." Indigenous materials and finishes contrast nicely with the contemporary finishes. Under the open, exposed corrugated metal ceiling filled with pipes and ducts—all

painted white—the marmoleum floor is finished in off-white and patterned with 4' x 8' inlays of a deeper beige. The wall and floor units are mostly natural beech wood, light and warm, accented with off-white laminated counter tops. Suspended from the ceiling are high bay luminaires in milk glass shades as well as floating panels or dropped "ceilings" of the natural beech wood. Some of

these elements carry the low voltage halogen lamps on tracks recessed within the accenting unit.

The walls are divided into bays by vertical fins and every second bay is highlighted by a pewter-finished, wrought iron sign holder and an oval, product identifying sign. MR16 lamps are contained in the metal arm to accentuate the attached sign. Some of the areas in the shop, like

DESIGN ◆ International Design Group, Toronto, ON

PROJECT TEAM ◆ David Newman & Ron Mazereeuw

MILLWORK/FIXTURES/CUSTOM CASES ◆ Verly Construction

REFRIGERATOR CASES/COOLERS ◆ Rapid Refrigeration

SIGNAGE ◆ LCBO Marketing

LIGHTING ◆ Juno Lighting

PHOTOGRAPHY ◆ Richard Johnson, Interior Images

"Vintages" at the rear of the space, are accented by tracks of MR16 lamps. The "Beer-Biere" section is further delineated by being finished in off-white instead of the beech wood. Since "Vintages" wines are truly the upscale items, they are given a special display treatment with single bottles featured in semi-circular extensions protruding out from the wall.

The designers, International Design Group of Toronto, created floor units that are adaptable and there are also simple beech boxes that can be stacked or used inside the floor units. Shopping carts are conveniently and neatly stocked near the entrance and the cash/wrap desk is located under a grill of pewter-finished ironwork. "This attention to detail creates an impressive backdrop and underscores the quality of the merchandise and creates a friendly and welcoming shopping experience."

LCBO MILLENNIUM KIOSK
Sherway Garden, Toronto, ON

The LCBO, in order to take advantage of the seasonal and holiday promotions, commissioned the International Design Group of Toronto to design a Millennium kiosk which would take up no more than ten feet by 20 feet of aisle space in malls, shopping centers and other heavily trafficked areas such as airports. These kiosks were to be self-contained units, easily locked and easily maintained. It was necessary—within the space restrictions—to provide as much storage and display room as possible.

Because of the space restraints, all displayers and showcases serve as selling and storage areas as well. The design is modular and flexible in concept so that kiosks can be designed from the available building units to suit a variety of spaces. The kiosks are thus easily assembled and can be readily dismantled and set up in a new space. The modules can be moved in or out and rearranged depending upon the stock and the space. Quality white birch wood is used for the cabinetry and reflects LCBO's high standards. It is the same look that appears in LCBO's freestanding stores. The lighting and signage is simple, direct and the kiosk is readily identified and recognized in the mall's traffic aisle. To reduce the bulkiness of the modules, decorative mesh with back-illuminated plexiglas is used to soften the case appearance.

The units shown here are located in Sherway Garden, Toronto—a busy, upscale mall. The unit here consists of a "circle" of showcases surrounding two interior display units capped by a wooden canopy. The upper portion of the showcases are used to display the available bottles of wine and the lower portion contains the stock. The corner elements as well as the two interior cases serve as extra storage cabinets. The corner pieces also hold changeable graphics or promotional posters. The suspended framework over the display cases house incandescent lamps while the showcases below are illuminated with fluorescents. The overall ambient light comes from the mall lighting.

DESIGN ✦ International Design Group, Toronto, ON
DESIGN TEAM ✦ David Newman & Ron Mazereeuw
GENERAL CONTRACTORS ✦ Salwood General Construction, Missisaugua, ON
WHITE BIRCH CABINETRY ✦ Salwood
LIGHTING ✦ Juno Lighting
BRUSHED ALUMINUM ✦ Octolam
DECORATIVE MESH ✦ Unalloy IWRC
PHOTOGRAPHY ✦ Richard Johnson, Interior Images

TESCO WINE SHOP
Tesco Supermarkets, UK

Tesco, a leading chain of supermarkets in the UK, was not satisfied with how their Wine & Spirits departments looked or functioned. They wanted to clearly define the departments and the products while creating a more enjoyable shopping experience for their clients.

The RPA design team of Columbus, OH was invited to create a strategy that would give the drink department "an individual character, providing an exciting and informative shopping experience." The new design organizes the whole department into logically segmented areas rather than an unending wall of wines

and beers. Feature promotional or focal points were added to direct the shopper's eye toward select ranges and products " adding interest and making the environment more stimulating." A flexible "promotional end" was also built into the design which can be either fully stocked during heavy shopping periods or converted simply

DESIGN ◆ RPA (Retail Planning Associates)
Columbus, OH

into a wine tasting counter for special events and promotions. Clear messages, in the area, stress "the importance of quality, authenticity and value," while providing the discerning shopper with basic background information about the products.

Muted Mediterranean colors are used on the walls and they serve as the background for the decorative elements, props and visual displays that add interest and warmth to the area. The fixtures that were used in the new wine area have a rustic look with wood front facings around the promotional area. The area is divided into wine regions and types of beers. A substantial number of pre-existing fixtures were incorporated into the new design concept.

Since the prototype was introduced shoppers seem to be drawn to the space; they stay longer and buy more. Only one month after the installation there was a 20% increase in wine sales. This design is currently being rolled out in all the new Tesco stores as well as in the refits.

R. FIELD WINE CO.
Honolulu, HI

The 1100 sq.ft. wine/spirits shop is actually a shop-within-the supermarket. The challenge for AM Partners of Honolulu was to create and maintain the R. Field Wine Co. as a distinct name and image even though it is part of a larger retail setting.

The designers conceived the space as a European country kitchen where the hand-picked, vine ripened produce, specialty deli and fine wines can be displayed. A rustic trellis, sandblasted and then stained, is suspended over the checkerboard patterned floor which further enhances the kitchen setting. The trellis helps to separate this shop from the surrounding supermarket

while also making this space seem more intimate and friendly. Light tracks are secured along the trellis "to provide a quiet excitement and show each of the specialty goods in the best light." It is the accent lighting and the warm, inviting colors that distinguish the space. Wines are stored in used wine cases that are enhanced with flutes and other details. Fresh produce surrounds the wine displays.

Along the inside wall there is a cheese cooler, humidor and a locked cabinet of fine, vintage wines. Shoppers are invited to meander through the space that is filled with assorted food specialties. "While accommodating the expectations of

loyal customers, it was also important for the store to be inviting to a new crowd of Epicureans."

MR16 lamps add sparkle to the wines and bottled goods while color corrected fluorescent lamps provide the general illumination and ensure the right presentation for the other products. Wines are also on display in other areas of the supermarket along wall racks and in special cases and as "accents" atop cases. The custom made fixtures are constructed of white oak and are stained two colors for variety and interest.

DESIGN ◆ AM Partners, Inc., Honolulu, HI

PROJECT ARCHITECT ◆ Charles Lau, Principal

PROJECT MANAGER ◆ Robert Domingo

PROJECT DESIGNER ◆ Louw Strydom

SPECIALTY CASES/FIXTURES ◆ Agarmate Display Cases

LIGHTING CONSULTANT ◆ Con Tech Lighting, Northbrook, IL

PHOTOGRAPHY ◆ Gary Hofheimer

DEAN & DE LUCA WINE ROOM
Charlette, NC

Like the satellite concept developed by Little & Associates Architects of Charlotte, NC for Dean & De Luca Market/Café, the design firm's Food Service Division came up with this small Wine Room concept. With the wine sales quite strong in the main Dean & De Luca store in Charlotte, this 1800 sq. ft. space not only is a retail wine shop and bar but it is also an attractive alternative for wine connoisseurs looking for a change from the usual bars for after dinner drinks and desserts.

The space has been designed to suggest a New York City Soho loft. It is painted white and has natural maple fixtures added along with architectural details. There are hardwood floors and woven chairs in beige and black. Black is used as a striking accent color in this high ceilinged space. The main decor is the display of over 600 labels in stock. A 250 sq. ft. mezzanine maximizes the use of the floor space and the more elite labels are showcased up here. The mezzanine rests on black enameled columns and it is trimmed with a black metal railing.

A baby grand piano—up front and near one of the gracious windows—provides entertainment at night. The black granite topped bar draws customers to the elegantly designed, stainless steel wine tap fixtures which serve up 48 different wines. Some of the fabulous Dean & De Luca desserts are on display in the stainless steel case that is adjacent to the wine bar.

DESIGN ◆ Little & Associates Architects, Charlotte, NC
FOOD SERVICE DIVISION ◆ Steve Starr & Josh Cool
REFRIGERATION CONSULTANT ◆ Clive Samuels & Assoc., Princeton, NJ
PHOTOGRAPHY ◆ Stanley Capps, Charlotte, NC

BRUNO'S GOURMET WINE CENTER
Bruno's Supermarket, Atlanta, GA

The Gourmet Wine Center is a small but strategically located shop within the 70,000 sq.ft. Bruno's Supermarket. This area, part of the total design created by Programmed Product Corp. of Plymouth, MI, is bordered by two facing walls of richly stained, mahogany colored wood which reach up to about seven feet in height and a pair of decorative arches at either end. Along the free standing walls the wines are shown on shelves and in cubicles within these library-like bookcase units. The elaborate custom fixtures and displayers define and create an image for this distinctive shop.

The objective of the design of the supermarket was "to provide the customer with a store thats environment and merchandising achieve a higher level than the area's competition." The pair of "Arches of Triumph" are made of the same deep colored wood and they flaunt cornices that tower over the surrounding semi-walls and serve as beacons for this department. They also set the theme and the look for the Gourmet Wine Center. The barrel vaulted interiors of the arches serve as stock support for the upscale, vintage wines. Behind and beyond the arches—in the center of the area—is a full round combination counter/wine tasting table/display unit where the wine steward is located. Here, the wine shopper can get information about which wines go with which foods, all about vintages, price ranges, wine growing areas and such.

DESIGN ◆ Programmed Products Corp., Plymouth, MI
Llew Reszka, President., PPC
FOR BRUNO'S ◆ Morrell Dodd, VP Engineer & Construction
CUSTOM MILLWORK/FIXTURES ◆ Southern Store Fixtures, Inc., Bessemer, AL
REFRIGERATION UNITS/COOLERS ◆ Hussmann, Bridgeton, MO
ORNAMENTAL WOOD ◆ Decorative Supply Corp., Chicago, IL
PHOTOGRAPHY ◆ Courtesy of PPC

WEIN & CO.
Vienna, Austria

The new wine shop/bar, located next to Vienna's Central Market and several theaters, is the work of Umdasch Shop Concept of Amstetten, Austria. The Central Market is a spectacular tourist attraction and Wein & Co. affords visitors the opportunity to taste a wide range of high level, international and local wines as well as gourmet specialties. After enjoying these delicacies at the bar the guest can tour the adjacent market where the products are available to-go.

The curved glass front—reminiscent of a wine keg updated and transparent—is all stainless steel and glass and opens into a foyer. Here a central display case introduces Wein & Co. and its product offering. The displayer also serves as a partial screen for the active counter/bar just beyond it. The total space is divided into two areas: the wine shop/market is on the left and the wine bar/counter is on the right. Slick black laminated cases and counters are featured in the bar and some of the walls are also painted black. The prep area, behind the bar, combines the black with stainless steel and the stainless steel also accents the counters/cases and the yellow/gold upholstered bar stools. The prepared salads and desserts are visible in the glass covered cases set between the white laminate topped counters. Here, the floor consists of terrazzo squares of several shades of beige.

Bright yellow gold floors appear throughout the wine selling and market part of the store and wood floor and wall units combine a light natural wood with wood that has been stained strong yellow and burgundy.

In addition to the wines displayed there is a mini-gourmet treat area where shoppers can pick up special snacks or pre-packaged specialty foods. The merchandise is neatly arranged on the yellow/gold wall system and the signage on top—in light yellow and burgundy—indicates which items are located where. The product signage throughout the market area continues the yellow/burgundy color scheme.

In Wein & Co. the designers have created "the successful mix of wine shop and bar as a meeting place for bon vivants of wines of the upper class."

DESIGNER ◆ Umdasch Shop Concept, Amstetten, Austria
FIXTURES/CASES/WALL SYSTEMS ◆ Umdasch
PHOTOGRAPHY ◆ Courtesy of Umdasch Shop Concept, Amstetten

COFFEE BEANERY
Little Rock, AR

Jo-Anne Shaw, founder and president of The Coffee Beanery, franchises which have been around for over a quareter of a century, was looking for some "pizzazz" in her stores. "I wanted a designer to take the look of our stores up a notch and give The Coffee Beanery the feel of an upscale, comfortable specialty coffee shop." She wanted a look that would be memorable: something that would focus on coffee and have longevity. Jo-Anne Shaw found her solution in the new design created by Zakaspace of Ft. Lauderdale, FL. Spiros Zakas, co-founder and chief of design for Zakaspace says, " Even before entering the store, the subtle

aroma of fresh brewed coffee is apparent." Once inside, the customer finds him or herself in another place and time. It is as though he or she may have traveled miles to some foreign and exotic coffee growing plantation in the Dutch

DESIGN ◆ Zakaspace, Ft. Lauderdale, FL
DESIGN TEAM ◆ Spiros Zakas, Chief of Design
PROJECT DESIGNERS ◆ Sarah Moran & Pamela Lieber
CERAMIC WALL TILE ◆ Dal Tile
SLATE FLOOR ◆ Impex Development, LLC
CARPETING ◆ Maisland Carpet
WALLCOVERING ◆ Vivacious
PENDANT LIGHTING ◆ Leucos Lighting
PHOTOGRAPHY ◆ Kelly Quinn

in Little Rock, the walls are covered with a basket weave print and also a fine printed design of banana leaves in subtle tones of green and gold. The fans that whir overhead and add to the tropical ambiance are equipped with natural palm leaf blades that complement the dark cherry wood used on the booths and table tops, and the animal prints in beige, gold and brown used to upholster the backs and seats.

"When customers walk in, the design directs their focus to the front service counters and the refrigerated cases so they can see the products and the various types of beans," says Zakas. Above the counters are brass-bound clocks set in the crown cherry wood soffit and the clocks are set with the times of major coffee growing regions. The wall below the clocks is clad with café au lait colored ceramic tiles.

All around the store and in the seating area there are decorative elements that recall the heritage of coffee from the banana leaves patterned on the wall covering which recalls the use of these trees to shade the coffee

West Indies or maybe even in far-off Morocco. You almost feel as though you have arrived at where the beans were grown and that you are about to savor the coffee or purchase it, perchance to brewing it at a time.

The "opening statement" consists of eight foot tall coffee trees clustered together on African slate floors and rich, handsome wood seems to be everywhere. In the center of the store is a display build-up of vintage luggage upon which the prepackaged coffees are displayed in a most atmospheric manner. Classic, English-style tables and even old-fashioned hand carts are used to enhance the presentation of the coffees and the coffee accessories. In the prototype store, a 2000 sq.ft. space

plants, to the dark woods associated with tropical regions. Zakaspace is currently updating other franchise locations to conform with this new look. Though the stores may vary from 100 sq.ft. to 3000 sq. ft., the new look in flooring, wall covering and tile work will be basic to each location. "The new design has been really great for us," says Ms. Shaw.

"The Zakaspace design team has developed a universal theme which has the look of yesteryear coupled with the mystique of the Colonial era. By incorporating accessories that are timeless and enduring, this design is easily adaptable to every Coffee Beanery location."

COFFEE PEOPLE
Denver, CO

To set themselves apart from the myriad caffeine and conversation operations that seem to be spreading across the world, Coffee People approached RPA of Columbus to create a coffee vending/coffee house inspired by the 1960s "Beat Culture" which espoused "romantic values, such as tolerance, inclusiveness and individualism." The RPA design firm created this Denver location which "combines tongue-in-cheek humor with civic courtesy and responsibility positioning itself for a young, culturally curious and highly educated consumer."

The color palette is warm and bright: it is fun, carefree, friendly and inviting. A rich yellow gold covers most of the walls and the stained and painted concrete floor is aswirl in patterns of red and blue. The service counter makes a bold statement by being banded in lavender, pale yellow and a salmon-red on top. Translucent blue and green spirals of fabric covered wire forms float overhead.. For the in-house coffee consumer there are three seating options: for the in-a-hurry, grab-and-go customer there are the bars along the window with

DESIGN ✦ RPA, Columbus. OH

DESIGN TEAM ✦ Doug Cheesman, CEO
  Diane Perduk Rambo: Creative Director
  Jeff Mc Call: Strategy Director
  Marie Haines: Planner/Merchandiser
  Perry Kolick: Lighting Design
  Charles Mindigo: Visual Communications

FIXTURES & FURNISHINGS ✦ Lowenstein,
  Pompano Beach, FL/Cipra & Frank, Berkley,
  CA/Thonet, Statesville, NC/Beverly
  Furniture, Pico Riviera, CA/Bermis Casual
  Furniture, Sheboygan, WI

SPECIAL FINISHES ✦ Pratt & Lambert and Optic
  Nerve Art Corp.

PHOTOGRAPHY ✦ Christian Deuber & Michael
  Houghton

pull-up stools. The Rendezvous Zone is centered under the swirling element hanging from the ceiling and a giant red dot on the floor. Here, black arm chairs are pulled up to the red topped tables. Afternoon imbibers can settle in for a pleasant chat in the overstuffed sofas and chairs provided for those who will stay awhile.

In a self-contained zone, in the rear of the space, is a sweeping piece of curved cabinetry that shows off the 24 different coffee blends avail-

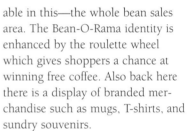

able in this—the whole bean sales area. The Bean-O-Rama identity is enhanced by the roulette wheel which gives shoppers a chance at winning free coffee. Also back here there is a display of branded merchandise such as mugs, T-shirts, and sundry souvenirs.

Consistent with the new retail identity program, designed by RPA, are the "retro-kitchy" visual communications and menu boards that entertain while they educate the consumer about the different beans and roasts. A community board, in keeping with Coffee People's "democratic spirit," is provided and customers can display notices about events or even items of personal interest. According to Diane Perduk Ramkbo, Creative Director at RPA eight guiding design principles were established to make this design true to the company's philosophy: "Stand for Something"; "Maintain Irony"; "Suspend Reality"; "Grow Whole Bean Sales"; "Accommodate Kids"; "Invite & Educate"; "Remove Tension" and "Maintain Mystery."

CC's COFFEE HOUSE,
New Orleans, LA

Architectural Interiors of New Orleans was commissioned by the Community Coffee Co., Ltd. to convert an existing bank building on Prytenia St. in New Orleans into a warm, friendly coffee retail operation and local coffee stop. Community Coffee has been in existence for over 80 years so the designers wanted to establish a look "rich in tradition, yet upscale and appealing to the younger target market." The finished 2000 sq,ft. space has the feeling of having been around since the early 1900s and that was accomplished by the design team's choice of colors, materials and motifs.

The soaring height of the original bank adds dignity and classic elegance to the space. This was enhanced by the warm, vanilla flavored walls which are accented with sage green and burgundy. Special millwork was designed for the store and it was executed in rich, mahogany stained oak. Special cabinetry was also designed to display and merchandise the 40 or more different gourmet coffees that are pre-bagged and available for immediate purchase. The displays and the displayers were all fashioned to make the product offering more accessible to the shoppers.

The CC's logo is embedded in the sisal carpet up front and also on the weathered wood sign board on the deep fascia facing the entering shopper. The balance of the floor is concrete stained in two shades of beige and patterned in an askew checkerboard design. To either side of the entrance are mahogany stained displayers that combine shelves with cabinet space below. Further back into the store, under a dropped ceiling, are displays of the pre-packaged coffees, the illuminated dessert case with a curved glass front and a service counter. The back wall or prep area is just beyond and burgundy laminated service units and work counters are

DESIGNER ◆ Architectural Interiors, New Orleans, LA
DESIGN TEAM ◆ Stephen Calamia: Project Architect
    Stephen Calamia & Shannon Parker
LIGHTING CONSULTANT ◆ Jerry Sarradet
CABINETS/MILLWORK/DISPLAYERS
    ◆ Architectural Wood Products.
REFRIGERATED CASES ◆ Millrock
WALL SHELVING ◆ Designer Metal Works
SIGNAGE/GRAPHICS/SPECIAL FINISHES ◆ Robert Lee
PHOTOGRAPHY ◆ Ron Calamia

located next to the warm, off-white wall.

Adding to the "old fashioned" ambiance are the turning, mahogany stained, wood-bladed, fans. Contemporary light fixtures were used "to give an upscaled style and to balance the traditional style of the millwork." Crown moldings and cornices around the soffit of the dropped ceiling complement the modern coffered pattern of the acoustical tiled ceiling.

COFFEE COMPANY
Amsterdam, The Netherlands

Rick Bekkema and Dick de Koch are coffee lovers. In addition to their own addiction to fine coffee they are entrepreneurs. The result is the Coffee Company which "introduces a new way of drinking coffee to Amsterdam." Not only are the high quality, gourmet blended coffees available for direct consumption, the coffee is also offered "to-go" which creates a very New York atmosphere. The imported, home roasted and freshly ground coffees, many from small specialized plantations, are also offered prepackaged in the shop. In very short order the Coffee Company formula has proven successful and three additional shops were opened in just over a year.

To create the retail environment the owners selected Concrete Architectural Associates, a young and spirited design firm. The designers selected four materials which they felt "worked with" the coffee: steel, wood, glass and stone. These materials were selected because, to the architects, they represented "pure, authentic, long-lasting, environment-friendly and customer-friendly." Gillian Schrofer of the design firm says that they did not focus on a target group. Rather they "translated the fine product of coffee into a store design" and that design is all about selling coffee. With direct input from Bekkema and de Koch, the Coffee Company is a "well balanced retail concept" that combines store design and

packaging with operational guidance and turn-over analysis. "A strong identity," says Rick Bekkema, "is combining all elements in your concept: in order to make yourself recognizable."

The long, narrow space is emphasized by the placement of the coffee service counter along one long perimeter wall. It is balanced by a very long, heavy timber topped table on the other side—along the window wall. Between the two, creating two traffic lanes, are two heavy, glass topped, stand-up counters. At the far end of the shop is a wall ablaze with assorted strong colored panels in which the special blends are presented.

The heavy timber floor planks and the rough textured, concrete

faced counter contrast with the stainless steel accents and the polished black stone counter top. Natural wood is also used to frame the windows. The unusually long and bulky table that can seat 22 seems to contradict all ideas about seating in a coffee shop. It actually makes strangers sit next to one another and "forces the customer into a more socially interactive role." "Inconsistency is tolerated as long as it contributes to a feeling as to what your company is about."

Currently more Coffee Company outlets are being built as well as smaller versions which are appearing in shopping malls and on shopping streets. One of these is also shown here.

DESIGNER ◆ Concrete Structural Associates, Amsterdam with Rick Bekkema & Dick de Koch
PHOTOGRAPHY ◆ Courtesy of Coffee Company

COFFEE REPUBLIC
London, UK

According to Fitch, the London based design firm that was responsible for the total new design package for the Coffee Republic, over the last several years "The branded retail category has been subject to significant growth and innovation." Though the Coffee Republic was successful, the growth of competition in the marketplace brought about the decision by management "to develop a second generation offer." This "offer" had to represent "an evolution from the current retaining a sense of familiarity for an already strong customer base."

After much research in the market, Fitch's design team came up with the " future personality" of Coffee Republic and translated that image into a new language of design and communication for the retail settings. The icon that now speaks for the company is an animated coffee cup and it can be seen on the packaging, menus, point of sale messages and the corporate literature. "A deliberate effort has been made to help people learn the language of coffee and to individualize the customer's experience and enjoy-

ment of visiting Coffee Republic." The coffee "Lingo Wall" in the retail store highlights the different types of coffee available and invites customers to try new combinations.

The interior is rich and coffee colored with lots of red mahogany colored wood cabinetry and mill-work. The menu boards are also deep brown while the floors are a combination of light, mottled tiles that accentuate the walk aisle and natural timber laid in the sitting

area. The front end of the shop has windows facing the street and is, therefore, the lighter, brighter part of the shop. Here the walls and ceiling are café au lait and much creamier in feeling than the deeper, richer brew color of the rear seating area. However, from the window and any-where in the shop, the brightly illu-minated "Lingo Wall" talks out and can be "heard." With assorted angled, dropped ceiling panels and soffits, the space picks up an energy and sense of vitality which is enhanced by the reddish glints of the wood surfaces. Low voltage, MR16s are recessed into the dropped ceilings over the seating area as well as the main service counter which combines glass fronted and illuminated cases with a serve counter top. The coffee selections are all on view against the satin, stainless steel back wall.

"The belief in quality is sup-ported with the use of quality mate-rials such as stone, solid timber and steel; the effect of which allows you to enjoy a luxury ten minute coffee experience."

ESPRESSO BAR MENU

		SHORT	TALL
ESPRESSO	single or double shot	0.90	1.20
ESPRESSO MACCHIATO	espresso + a dollop of foamed milk	0.90	1.20
ESPRESSO CON PANNA	espresso + whipped cream	1.05	1.35
CAPPUCCINO	espresso + steamed milk + foamed milk	1.20	1.45
CAFFE LATTE	espresso + steamed milk	1.20	1.45
CAFFE MOCHA	espresso + steamed milk + hot chocolate + whipped cream	1.45	1.70
CAFFE AMERICANO	espresso + hot water	0.90	1.20
ICED CAFFE AMERICANO			1.30
ICED CAFFE LATTE			1.50
ICED CAFFE MOCHA			1.70
FREEZER	ice blended cool and creamy		1.95

DESIGNER ◆ Fitch, London

DESIGN TEAM ◆ John Harrison: CEO/Project Leader
Carol Dean and Nick Richards: Senior Graphic Designers

PHOTOGRAPHY ◆ Tim Goffe/Robert Howard

GOODBEAN COFFEE
Brighton, UK

Goodbean Coffee Cafés are opening around England and besides offering a wide range of gourmet coffee beans to-go, they also offer a "bright, uplifting environment" in which to enjoy a selected brewed beverage. Rather than resort-ing to the usual dark, rich coffee colors that are frequently used to promote premier coffees, John Herbert Partnership of London, the architects/designers of the 1800 sq.ft. shop in Brighton, opted for "bright primary colors to reflect the seaside origins of the brand: the sun, sky and the sea." The designers mixed quick-visit seating on stools at counters with comfortable couches to "provide a bustling, people-watching zone."

The good time and the Goodbean experience begin out front. Red canvas awnings cap the spacious windows and the outdoor furniture combines red, white and blue for the chairs and tables. John Herbert Partnership also designed the new logo which first

appears out front and the graphics as well as the product packaging. According to John Herbert, "The 'G' bean mark (the Company's icon) has humour. We wanted to avoid the stereotypical steaming coffee cup."

Inside the store the walls are bright red and sunny yellow and the

DESIGNER/ARCHITECT ◆ John Herbert Partnership, London

DESIGN TEAM ◆ John Herbert/Neil Bedford/Kevin Owen

LIGHTING CONSULTANT ◆ Aktiva, London

MILLWORK/CABINETRY/FIXTURES ◆ Woodland Shopfitters, Harlow

WALL SYSTEM ◆ Woodland Shopfitters as to JHP design

REFRIGERATED CASES ◆ Provided by client

GRAPHICS/SIGNAGE ◆ JHP

PHOTOGRAPHY ◆ Keith Parry, London

custom cases are laminated in a deep blue. Deep blue signboards, with white lettering, are layered atop the yellow walls and the products, in their bright and sunny packages, are positioned "strategically throughout the purchase and consumption area" on stainless steel fixtures designed by JHP. The white ceilings add to the light and airy feeling of the shop as do the light-weight metal tables and chairs; the same as those used outside. To the right, upon entering, is a tempting patisserie display case and a service counter where coffee is served and money accepted. A servery is

located at the end of this line. Opposite is another rounded glass case in which prepared gourmet sandwiches are shown. This is followed by the condiment server. The tables are set out on the slate tiled floor and beside the windows there is some bar and stool seating. From here one can watch the people parade on Nile St. and Meeting House Lane.

The original prototype store, shown here, has been very successful and another Brighton location was soon added. Several others are planned as the brand name and product recognition increases.

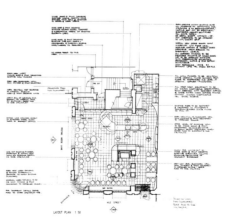

LAYOUT PLAN 1:50

T-BAR
Baker St., London, UK

Whittard of Chelsea has a long and notable reputation as a tea and coffee merchant in the UK. The firm has many free-standing shops where their teas and coffees are sold along with coffee makers, tea pots, cups and saucers and the sundry accessories that go with the brewing and savoring processes. With the explosion of coffee bars and the appearance of the U.S. coffee chains in the UK, Whittard of Chelsea called upon Carte Blanche of London to come up with a new take-away concept with an emphatically British menu of hot and iced teas and coffees. These

would be complemented by a changing seasonal selection of mince pies and pastas in the cooler months and cucumber sandwiches in the summer.

The interior reflects a warm palette of natural stone and strip wood flooring along with beech wood bar and stools and stainless steel counter—all in a crisp off-white envelope. The bright and major accent color is the vibrant blue that is Whittard's signature color. It appears out front on the canvas awnings that in the warmer months offers shelter from the sun at the tables set out on the street. Inside there is the bright blue glass mosaic tiling that faces the service bar and the supporting columns, on the floor, are finished in the same color. Colored piers on the wall serve as giant frames for displays of fresh fruits. The wall behind the service counter is cubby-holed with squares in which pre-packaged teas are shown. Over 100 varieties of teas

are on sale here. The floor pattern directs shoppers from the entrance to the self-selection area and then onto the hot foods and finally to the tea and coffee selection point.

The t-Bar caters to seasonal and menu changes as well as interior mood changes. The lighting has been designed so that the ambient "mood" can be altered seasonally just as the seating can be moved out into the sunshine for an open air

DESIGNER ◆ Carte Blanche, London, UK
CONTRACTOR ◆ Interior PCC
FIXTURES/FITTINGS ◆ Dean & Bowes
GRAPHICS ◆ Bostock & Pollitt
PHOTOGRAPHY ◆ Adrian Wilson

brasserie feeling or contained within in nasty weather. In the winter the interior becomes more intimate and "warm" with the addition of cushions and an altered lighting plan. It is truly a t-Bar for all seasons.

T-ZONE
Carnaby St., London, UK

Situated in high traffic areas like Covent Garden and Carnaby St., is a new concept store from Whittard of Chelsea. It is the t-Zone. In an environment that is cool, calm and relaxing, customers can expand their knowledge and also experience the huge variety of available teas. As designed by Carte Blanche of London, there is a promotional "tasting pod" where shoppers can try new products. For the more adventurous there is a long central blending table with stainless steel bowls displaying mixed tea leaves, herbs and flowers that can be added to a selection of other teas. Here shoppers can create their own mixes—aided by a recipe wheel which recommends compatible blends. The customer can then "package" her creation and finish it off with a personalized label.

Shown here is the Carnaby setting which combines natural timber floors with flat white walls and ceiling to form a neutral backdrop for the simple, lightweight merchandising fixtures. Modular, silvery metal units hold display boxes that are fin-

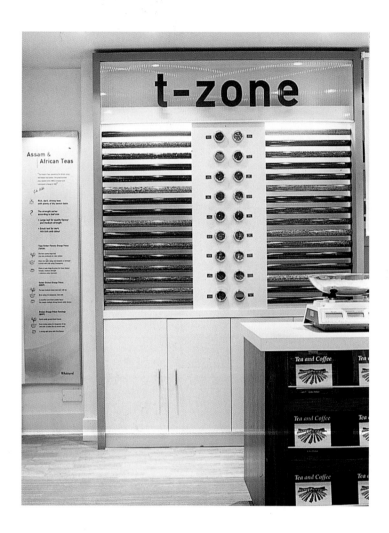

ished to directly reflect the strength of the teas. Light teas appear in off-white boxes, cool-green is the medium teas and the stronger teas are contained in boxes of rich, American walnut veneers. To make the selection process simpler, the tea categories are indicated on clear, reeded glass plaques. Between the fixtures are bold, vertical graphic panels that explain the origin of the tea, its characteristics and even the ideal brewing times.

"The t-Zone appeals to the senses through the highly visual display of tubes and tester pots showing the teas' diversity of leaf size, colors and textures combined with the mix of heady aromas. t-Zone offers a totally refreshing experience."

DESIGNER ◆ Carte Blanche, London, UK
CONTRACTOR ◆ Dean & Bowes
FIXTURES/CASES/MILLWORK ◆ Dean & Bowes
PHOTOGRAPHER ◆ Adrian Wilson

POUPON PATISSERIE
Washington, DC

Georgetown, the heart of the shopping/dining/browsing area of Washington, DC, was the location selected by the noted Baltimore baking company, Fresh Pastry, for their new bakery/café. The original 19th century commercial building was in poor condition but the client and the designers, George Gordon Architects of Washington, DC, saw "key characteristics that conformed to the spirit of the Baltimore Bakery."

The existing brick bearing walls—reminiscent of old brick ovens—were retained and cleaned "to provide a warm character and ideal counterpoint to the soft, organic shapes of the breads and pastries." To complement the old brick, the designers added stainless steel, glass and granite and all together they affect a delightful setting for the hand crafted cakes, tarts, beads and chocolates. The elaborate pastries are showcased in custom designed glass and steel cases. The under 1600 sq. ft. space also serves as an enjoyable place to stop for a cup of coffee-to go with the baked goods—and there is seating at an intimate coffee-bar at the rear of the space. The kitchen, upstairs, is reached by a new staircase which is highlighted by a modern, stainless steel aircraft railing.

The fortunate first-comers get to enjoy the freshly baked foods and brewed coffee in the open, curved glass window area in the front with its view out onto the busy street, the brick steps, and the brick laid patio out front with the changing plants. Inside the brick path continues from the doorway to the small café in the rear. Dark wood timber floors are laid where the tables are set and the new staircase is flanked by one of the old brick walls. The service wall, behind the sleek cases and counters, is partially tiled and the balance is a creamy white plastered wall. In a recessed area the old brick wall shows through to contrast with the stainless steel rod and natural wood shelf displayer system. The assorted breads are displayed in wicker baskets.

A beige/gray speckled granite acts as a work counter. Low voltage lighting is integrated into the three dimensional scheme not only to enhance the product presentation

DESIGNER ◆ George Gordon Architects, Washington, DC
George Gordon, Partner in Charge
MELANIE COTTLE ◆ Project Architect
PHOTOGRAPHY ◆ Andrew Lautman

but "to extend the design vocabulary of glass and stainless steel into the space of the café." According to George Gordon, the architect/designer, "The energy of the original shop in Baltimore has been transplanted to Washington and the result is a vibrant neighborhood bakery/café that provides a gathering place for this home design district of Georgetown."

STELLA BAKERY & CAFE
Peraso, Italy

The small city of Pesaro is home to Sifa, a world-wide known designer/manufacturer of fixtures and fittings for specialty food stores and fashion retailing. As a showcase for their new Star #2 line of metallic wall systems and floor fixtures, Sifa commissioned Studio Garbugli & Vincenzetti to create this upscale, fresh and contemporary bakery and café in a 6000 sq. ft. space in Pesaro.

The palette is light and neutral: a perfect setting for the rich, warm colors of the crusty breads, the braided beauties and the assorted festive cakes that are presented on wall units and in the glass fronted floor cases. Light colored wood insets contrast with the baked metal and the neutral plastic laminates used on the case fronts and the wall system that lines the walls. The floor is covered with a large scale, light beige ceramic tile and the exposed walls are faux painted in a tone on tone texture accented with bands of blue. A partial wall separates the retail bakery from the café/bar and prepared antipasti and some ready-to-go light snacks are shown in the glass fronted case that faces the café. Adding a homey touch is the frieze above with a collection of hand painted plates on display.

Packaged specialties are shown on a light colored wood fixture with rounded shelves while more breads are available for self-select from the wood faced units along the wall. These combine angled viewing with flat lay-down of product. The upper shelves are tilted for better viewing and accessibility and a mirrored panel, behind the uppermost shelf, shows off the piled up breads to full advantage. Sweeping out from each four foot wide wall module is a light shield that keeps the light that illuminates the product from getting into the shopper's eyes.

DESIGNER ◆ Studio Garbugli & Vicenzetti, Pesaro, Italy
FIXTURES & FITTINGS ◆ Star #2 by Sifa, SPA, Pesaro
MILLWORK/CABINETRY ◆ Sifa
SHELVING/WALL UNITS ◆ Sinthesi, SRI
GRAPHICS ◆ Studio 33
PHOTOGRAPHY ◆ Studio 33, Pesaro

MOZART
Toronto, ON, Canada

According to Diego Burdi and Paul Filek, the partners and creative directors of Burdifilek of Toronto, the design of the 750 sq. ft. Mozart "began with a vision of an old world patisserie experience in the context of modern, uptown Toronto." The designers were brought in "to create a unique space to showcase the pastry creations and shape a cross-cultural ambiance."

The experience begins upon entering the shop and the customer faces an array of fabulous pastries and a wall of cookies. A rolled, dropped ceiling dramatizes the space and "adds intimacy to the experience." The color palette is based on the baked goods being presented

and it ranges from meringue white to chocolate brown with a neutral mauve in between. The sales counter is of white glass and self illuminated to glow in the space. It is banded with deep, rich brown stained ash wood. The cash/wrap counter, beyond the sales case, is finished in chocolate brown and topped with white. European flair and tradition is evident in the rounded display case set out on the precisely laid white floor tiles which are patterned with a grid of chocolate brown. The "cookie wall" is hand painted with circles in 20 pastel colors and this is where the pre-packaged goods are displayed floating on glass shelves. On the shop's pin-striped back wall lifestyle elements are introduced in the square niches. There are floral arrangements and various objects of interest including an orange George Nelson clock—"a witty reminder that the sweet creations offered here can be daily or hourly pleasures." A center recess in the rear wall features a mauve colored door with a porthole window and a limited view into the bakery beyond. Behind the main glass display case and overhung with custom metallic lighting fixtures are some oversized cake and pastry "sculptures" that tower in the illuminated, deep brown niche. "The overall effect (of the shop) is international and irresistible."

DESIGNER ◆ Burdifilek Design Team, Toronto, ON
    Diego Burdi: Design Director
    Paul Filek: Managing Partner
    Tom Yip & Cathy Knott: Designers
CONTRACTOR & MILLWORK ◆ Planit Construction
REFRIGERATED CASES ◆ Metropolitan Refrigeration
PROPS/DECORATIVES ◆ Teatro Verde
LIGHTING ◆ Eurolite
FLOORING ◆ Dal Tile
PHOTOGRAPHY ◆ Hasnain Dattu, Westside
    Studios, Toronto, ON

BREADLINE
Washington, DC

Located in metropolitan Washington, DC is an upscale bakery/café of 3500 sq.ft. designed by Core of Washington, DC. As the name implies and as the layout of the space indicates, the focus is on the bread-making and baking in the open bakery that can be viewed when seated at the standard height tables at the rear of the space. From the bar height area, the diner has a clearer view of the grill activity. What makes the space so noteworthy is the use of colors and materials. Functional concrete columns become palettes upon which ocher, mustard, olive and rust tones are blended and the floors, like the columns, are "canvases" for a modern painter. Bands of mottled and blended shades and tints of ocher, olive and persimmon stripe the floor horizontally to somewhat camouflage the long, narrow floor plan. The display cases and service counters are playfully and geometrically patterned—like Mondrian paintings—with natural maple panels stained green, olive, gold and terra cotta as well as left natural. The architect/designer calls this "the dis-

rhythmic paneling of the millwork." He also refers to the color scheme as having "a heartland feeling." The service counter, like the Espresso bar, is topped with zinc that harmonizes with the stainless accents of the machinery on the back wall.

In contrast to all the color saturated floors, columns and piers is the clean white finish of the walls and the curved, dropped ceiling over the service counter. According to Peter Hapstack of Core, "The wall surfaces are treated as gallery space and hold photographic depictions of people baking bread and enjoying good food."

1 HIGH SEATING AREA
2 LOW SEATING AREA
3 DISPLAY
4 MEN'S ROOM
5 WOMEN'S ROOM
6 STORAGE
7 OFFICE
8 SEATING
9 ELECTRICAL CLOSET
10 CONDIMENT STAND
11 ADA COMPLIENT RESTROOM
12 BAKERY
13 WASH AREA
14 COOLER
15 FREEZER
16 PREP AREA
17 ORDER LINE
18 COOKING
19 ESPRESSO COUNTER
20 DISPLAY CASES
21 OVEN

The lighting, like everything at Breadline, has a feeling of improvization about it. Using assorted shapes and sizes of light bulbs, the design-

ers have suspended them at assorted levels throughout the seating area. The same rich color palette is used here for the chairs and tables: the light, natural maple wood is stained in the same colors and then arranged in no logical order.

In addition to the breads artistically presented in straw baskets atop the counter and in the cases in front of the open-for-viewing bakery, there are bags of flour stacked up front on a rough wood palette. This introduces the bakery theme to the customer entering Bread line. The overall feeling of this multi-award winning bakery/café is "warm, bright and inviting."

DESIGNER ◆ Core, Washington, DC

PROJECT ARCHITECT ◆ Peter Hapstack, III, AIA, ISP

DESIGN TEAM ◆ Dale Stewart, AIA/Diana Horvat, RA/Christine K.Wan/Scott Klugel, AIA/Randll S. Seitz, AIA/Brent A. Campbell

MILLWORK ◆ Enterprise Woodcraft & Design, Inc. Silver Spring, MD

ENGIUNEER ◆ Metropolitan Engineering, Inc., Washington, DC

FOOD SERVICE ◆ Next Step Design, Annapolis, MD

PHOTOGRAPHY ◆ Maxwell Mac Kenzie, Washington, DC

BAKERY CAFE
Ontario Mills, CA

With a space of only 850 sq.ft., Bakery Café carries on the tradition and presents the same high quality associated with the Cheesecake Factory of which it is a new off-shoot. Not only are the ingredients of the same top quality but so is the design of this satellite shop located in the Ontario Mills shopping and entertainment center.

"Our goal was to set our Bakery Café apart from the crowd," says Rick McCormack, the in-house designer for The Cheesecake Factory. "Immediately your eyes notice our classic inspired storefront, fabricated of what appears to be carved limestone." A boldly colored oval sign straddles the wide opening into the shop and the small seating area up front.

Inside one is immediately embraced by the warmth exuding from the golden yellow walls and the hammered copper dye facings on the service counter and the self-illuminated cases filled with Cheesecake Factory famous dessert selections. Contrasting all this is the rich cherry wood of the soffit that underscores the mural frieze over the service line. The cherry wood also frames the polished copper cases which are capped with white marble. The specially commissioned mural is a composition of fruits, vegetables and cheeses rendered in deep, dramatic yet quite vibrant colors. Topping off the mural is a classic ornamented molding frieze in a verde gris finish. The coffered ceiling combines the same faux finish of the yellow gold walls with black plaster grille insets.

The decorative menu boards, contained in gold leafed frames, carry through the brown of the wood with lettering in gold. Accenting the side walls are oval framed, peach toned mirrors highlighted by ornate wall lighting fixtures that complement the special, custom, artist-blown glass pendants that follow the sweep of the counter. All together, the stage is set for the signature cheese cakes, desserts, gourmet coffee and espresso drinks.

DESIGNER ◆ Rick McCormack, VP Store Design, The Cheesecake Factory
MILLWORK/CABINETRY ◆ Westco
REFRIGERATED UNITS/COOLERS ◆ Federal
GRAPHICS/SIGNAGE ◆ Rio Design, Corporate Design
SPECIAL FINISHES/MURALS ◆ Michael Sapienza
LIGHTING DESIGN ◆ Rick McCormack
PHOTOGRAPHY ◆ Cameron Carothers

CHESAPEAKE BAGEL FACTORY
Atlanta, GA

The bright, sunny interior of the newly remodeled Chesapeake Bagel Factory is the result of a total design concept initiated and visualized by Creative Culinary Design, Inc. of Irvine, CA.

The 1700 sq.ft. space not only serves as a bakery for the never-ending supply of freshly baked bagels and breads, but also is a lively café where the baked goods can be munched on "as is" or as the bases for sandwiches along with soups and coffee drinks. From the new, light color tiled floors and the assorted seating alternatives in light maple with yellow/gold stained seats and the golden yellow service counter. Yellow is the color. It also appears as the sunny accent tiles on the prep area wall and on the faux painted walls, so it is always a bright "good morning" at the Chesapeake Bagel Factory. Complementing the "sunshine"—in the truest sense—is the dramatic sweep of purple fascia over

DESIGNER ◆ Creative Culinary Design, Inc., Irvine, CA

PROJECT DESIGN TEAM ◆ Adolf Pereira/David Lee/Angie Allen/Michael Owings/Frank A. Torres/Don De Bow

MURALS/ARTWORK/DECORATIVE SIGNAGE ◆ Michael Dula Design

PHOTOGRAPHY ◆ Courtesy of Creative Culinary Design

the black and white covered coffee counter on the left and the purple banners hanging from the ceiling between the various stations on the service line. The lower part of the wainscoted walls is finished in a fresh, lettuce-green color. A mural in vivid yellows, violets, greens, blues and black fills most of one of the perimeter walls over the fixed booth seating. The yellow stained chair backs are complemented by the purple upholstery.

In addition to the colorful signage over the service stations, there are tempting displays of breads and bagels, in straw baskets, behind the serving counter and also in a wood and metal shelf rack up near the window and adjacent to the counter and pull up stools that line the window wall. Paintings that relate to the mural—in color and style—add more spots of color to the space.

To quote the designer—and the client—"the change was dramatic!"

DONUT KING
Atlanta, GA

A donut may be a donut or a donut can become something special and unique. It can just be something to dunk in a cup of coffee—or a sweet alternative to a bagel. It can be given gourmet status when the dough is a low fat product that produces a less greasy donut while still retaining all the expected flavor. When a Korean emigre, Eui H. Sung developed this new donut formula and opened six different donut shops in Atlanta, he realized that he needed a brand identity because that is almost as important as the donut itself. "I wanted to develop a unique environment that would give a visual identity to the low fat, premium donut," said Mr. Sung.

Lorenc Design of Atlanta was selected to create the new brand image and the shop design that would sell the donut and also attract young minority couples to invest in franchising the name and the product. Chung Youl Yeo, an architect at Lorenc Design, faced with a 900 sq.ft. space and a very limited budget said, "We started with a contemporary style and incorporated icons that would be consistent with more shops." The designers were interested in creating a bistro-like or coffee shop setting rather than a fast-

foods look. Using paint, vinyl tile and lettering, laminates, metal chairs, a sense of humor and fresh clear colors—the prototype for Donut King evolved.

Looking in through the wide expanse of glass one is immediately drawn to the service counter with its yellow and white striped canopy. "The hole in the canopy is like the sun" and it is used to suggest the morning sun—the time when most shoppers stop at Donut King. The menu board, hanging through the opening, is like "an open eye." The floors are patterned with 12" x 12" vinyl tiles in gray, black and yellow that are custom cut in a striped design that seems to lead the shopper from the door to the counter. The walls are painted white, bright blue and sunny yellow. The white laminate table tops have internal "donut holes" of a gray laminate inlay and these are complemented by the donut backed red chairs made of stained wood on bent metal frames. Within the limited space 12-16 patrons can be accom-

DESIGNER • Lorenc Design, Atlanta, GA
PHOTOGRAPHY • Rion Rizzo/Creative Service

modated. Customers can also look into the kitchen/bakery through a viewing window accented with an acid etched logo.

The 2x4 dropped ceiling is custom painted gray and 2x4 fluorescent fixtures are set in a checkerboard in the ceiling. In addition, flood can lights are recessed in the long hallway. Lorenc not only designed the space but also custom designed the tables and chairs, the donut display case, self service coffee unit, the store front and the graphics and signage.

GODIVA CHOCOLATIER
Hong Kong

Creating the new global retail concept for Godiva Chocolatier, Desgrippes Gobe & Assoc. of New York City built on the art nouveau concept they had originally designed for the Godiva shops in the U.S. With their original design, more product was brought out from behind the counters and the walk-in refrigerated cases were developed. However, in

DESIGNER ◆ Desgrippes Gobe & Associates, New York, NY; David Ashen
DIRECTOR OF ARCHITECTURE ◆ Leyden Yaeger
MILLWORK/CABINETRY/FIXTURES ◆ Parisi, Royal, PA
REFRIGERATED CASES ◆ Parisi, Royal, PA
SPECIAL FINISHES/DISPLAYS ◆ Fresco Decorative Arts
PHOTOGRAPHY ◆ Custom, courtesy of Godiva Chocolatier, Hong Kong

other parts of the world different concepts of retailing take precedent as well as personal preferences. Some wanted to retain the original black and gold look while others wanted a more art deco look.

The marketing strategy that was developed retains Godiva's "sense of elegance and specialness" while losing "the exclusivity and intimidation" aspects. "Affordable Luxury" becomes the theme and presents the product not only as a chocolate for special occasions but also for more personal indulgence. According to the designers at Desgrippes Gobe & Assoc., "The design strategy was to directly communicate these brand equities through the retail environment while modernizing and revitalizing the existing store design concept."

The new "Modern Heritage" concept uses some of the original art nouveau concepts but has accommodated them to suit the

The display columns with gold line vitrines are illuminated from the top by MR16s. The wall cases fit in between the columns and they can be manufactured in three sizes, thus creating a kit of parts. The prepackaged boxes of chocolates are displayed in open refrigerated cases and customers are encouraged to interact directly with the products. The light cream, faux finished walls, the hardwood floors and the cherry wood and marble cabinetry and cases are all brightly illuminated in this 700 sq. ft. Hong Kong location. The architecture was "softened" with more curves and the whole design is less elaborate than that used in the U.S. "The luxury and sophistication associated with Godiva is highlighted but people aren't put off by the design. They find it warm and welcoming," says David Ashen.

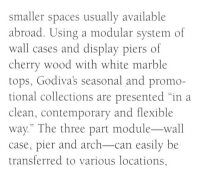

smaller spaces usually available abroad. Using a modular system of wall cases and display piers of cherry wood with white marble tops, Godiva's seasonal and promotional collections are presented "in a clean, contemporary and flexible way." The three part module—wall case, pier and arch—can easily be transferred to various locations,

types of stores and physical spacial layouts. The materials and details incorporated are reminiscent of the American prototype "to ensure worldwide brand image consistency. David Ashen, Desgrippes Gobe's director of architecture says, "With this system you can separate the ten different collections and highlight special items."

SEVEN ON STATE ST.
Marshall Field Dept. Store, Chicago, IL

The objective for Walker Group/CNI of New York, NY was to renovate Marshall Field's outdated food floor in the handsome, landmark building on State St. in Chicago. The request was to "create state-of-the-art interactive food and beverage facilities combined with retail" of gourmet and specialty food products.

To affect the desired look and use for the seventh floor, the design team focused on "the theatrical nature of preparing and selling food." The designers defined five individual food stations with open kitchens and these were related to retail facilities where shoppers can sample the various foods as well as purchase the ingredients. A series of sweeping, curved walls and counters create a dynamic setting for the food prep areas while the ingredients and equipment are showcased in niches. The palette for the floor is light and neutral with terrazzo flooring, mosaic tiles, woven metals (stainless, copper and brass), light beige covered walls and handsome, fixtures and cabinetry finished in white-rubbed pickle finish.

There is a large chocolate/candy area up on the seventh which is divided into a string of brand name boutiques. Here the wood wall cabinets with illuminated display niches and/or shelves feature the gift packaged merchandise. The glass counters display the chocolates from which the customers can create their

own gift packages. Among the famous confectioners on view are Joseph Schmidt, Neuhaus, and the Frango brand which has long been a Marshall Field exclusive.

In the Frango boutique smart tables are set out on the wood floor. They are made of a golden toned wood trimmed with stainless steel. The same wood is used for the simple, roll-about gondolas. The wall shelving units combine wood uprights with stainless steel edged shelves. A delightful oasis, in this area, is Frango Café. It is one of the several refreshment bars on Seventh.

DESIGNER ◆ Walker Group/CNI, New York, NY
    Jay Valgora: Design Principal
DESIGN TEAM ◆ Alan Ademac, RA/Steven
    Kitezh/Marcyle Wallman/Donald West/
FOR DAYTON HUDSON ◆ Jane Van Auken, Dir.
    Of Store Planning & Design
    Michael Tietz: Staff Srchitect
    Jamie Becker: Dir. of V.M..
MILLWORK/CABINETRY ◆ Bernhard
    Woodwork, Ltd.
REFRIGERATED CASES ◆ M.L. Rongo, Inc.
PHOTOGRAPHY ◆ Susan Kezon

Another favorite port of call is the classy and classic wine shop. Here, in a curved area dramatized by a dropped ceiling and a round column turned into a focal showcase for the department, the stock is arranged into horizontal cubby-holes along the curved wall. Floating shelves, between the rows of circular, cut-out openings, support a display of the wines contained in the openings above and below the shelves.

In addition to the new floor layout and the custom designed fixtures, Walker Group/CNI created the entire graphic design system that integrates the old and new architecture and also tells the Marshall Field story.

CANDY CAULDRON
Downtown Disney's West Side, Lake Buena Vista, FL

You can taste it before you even see it. You can smell it even though you are still outside. You know you want it because you are there. The wicked, ugly old witch, dipping her apple in the steaming cauldron, isn't going to frighten you away or lessen your desire for the treats you know are inside. From the dimensional "signage" and the wave-like canopy that meanders up and down across the shop front to the enticing window display, you know you are captive. You have no choice but to enter into the magical experience of Candy Cauldron, the new Disney retail shop in Disney's West Side in Lake Buena Vista, FL.

The design of this 1000 sq. ft. space of which only 600 sq.ft. is available for retail is the result of the combined efforts and talents of Ibarra Collaborative International, Inc., Pamela Temple Interiors, Walt Disney Attractions Inc. of Buena Vista and Walt Disney Imagineering of Glendale, CA. The space has "a storyline reflecting the indulgent environment that supports the experience of the West Side, and the smell of candy and the sounds of the laboratory enhance the experience."

The apple motif is introduced out front with the apple dipping witch and continues inside where the witch reappears holding a red apple while the wicked queen car-

ries a green apple. Since the space is so limited and 400 sq. ft. is used for the working candy-making kitchen, there is really only one major displayer/merchandiser and it sits in the middle of the ocher/gold stained concrete floor. The four sided, reinforced fiberglass unit combines the vines and apples motifs. The Queen and the Witch stand atop this focal unit.

The surrounding walls are cleverly painted with "stone" surfaces, arches, vanishing stairways, niches and alcoves—all to open up the space and also provide the right atmosphere for scenes from Disney's "Snow White" feature cartoon. "It helps orient the environment of the dungeon." Set within these simulated "stone arches" on one of the perimeter walls are more candy product displays. A refrigerated case displays chocolates and other "fragile" products. Overhead the ceiling is painted with a deep blue phosphorescent paint and black light is used to create the tumulous, stormy sky.

The same "dungeon" ambiance appears in the kitchen which is filled with stainless steel and copper pots, pans and kettles. It is a mix of old and new and fun to behold behind the expanse of glass window that separates it from the rest of the space. The candy apple dipping is part of the show!

DESIGNERS • Ibarra Collaborative
  International, Inc., Orlando, FL
  Pamela Temple Interiors, Orlando, FL
  Walt Disney Attractions, Inc., Lake Buena
  Vista, CA
  Walt Disney Imagineering, Glendale, CA
FIXTURES • PAM International, Inc., Saddle
  Brook, NJ
  RSP Production, Orlando, FL
  Westco, Inc. New York, NY
PHOTOGRAPHY • Courtesy of Walt Disney
  Prtoductions

SWEET CANDY
Karstadt, Hertie, Munich, Germany

Karstadt Warrenhaus AG is one of Europe's biggest companies and Karstadt Department Stores appear in most major cities in Germany. Realizing the potential of candy sales in the department store, the company entrusted Planungsburo von Baczko of Hamburg, with a space of 45 sq. meters in a Munich store in which to create a prototype design that could be tested, tweaked and then realized in 20 other department stores. Since the spaces and the shapes and sizes would vary, the designers came up with a modular design as shown here.

Targeted at the children—and the younger adults—Von Baczko came up with a bright, color-filled futuristic space theme that consists of gondolas that can be used flat against a perime-ter wall or used back to back to become a double sided, middle-of-the-space shelved gondola. The modules can be accessorized with shelves, drawers or pour-outs. The green drawers are heavily textured and pro-duced by a vacuum forming process. Bright colored laminates veneer the sides and they are trimmed with alu-minum edging. The design concept also includes a full-round, space ship shaped unit that combines dump with shelves. The cash/wrap desk is also modular. It consists of seg-mented arcs and depending upon the allotted space—more or less arcs can be used. Each segment is made up of brushed aluminum frames filled with green plexiglass panels sandwiched with perforated tin plate. These pan-els are illuminated from behind caus-ing the desk to glow. The big red heart, over the desk, is visible from a distance and it is the distinguishing Sweet Candy department signage. According to the designer, " Through the mist of a fog producing machine, the rays of light penetrate through the perforated surface of the heart, like long feelers groping through the

DESIGNER ◆ Plasnungsburo von Baczko,
  Hamburg
  Volker von Baczko: Principal
  Andrea Schmitt: Interior Architect
  Uwe Teichert & Dieter Lakowitz: Design
  Team
  Michael Fritz: Graphic Designer
  Nicola Schaller: Illustrator
FIXTURES ◆ Designed by von Baczko and pro-
  duced by Karstadt Warrenhaus AG, Munich
PHOTOGRAPHY ◆ Andreas Borowsky

room." Controls, located at the desk, are used to adjust the basic lighting, the gobo projections, neon outlines, displays and the heart illumination as well as the aforementioned fog and sound machines.

To keep with the lime green, yellow and orange color scheme, shovels shaped like green frogs are available to the candy customers who want to fill their own bags. Changing gobo projections on the heart, 3D effects, illuminated panels, aluminum tails and fins, neon outlines and shiny surfaces all intensify the illusion that the shopper is being served by Princess Leah in some far-away, out of space station.

FANNY MAY
Bollingbrook, IL

The new brand look and image for Fanny May Candies was designed by Frankel Brand Environments of Chicago, IL. Although the Fanny May brand promise was "freshness guaranteed," that promise was missing in the look of their retail stores. Through category signage, merchandising and fixture design, Frankel faced the challenge of realizing the promise in the new prototype retail store built in Bollingbrook, IL.

Since Fanny May outlets can appear in malls, in shopping centers, as free-standing stores on retail streets or even as vendor shops in other retail operations, Frankel's new design concept is modular. The new fixtures, display tables and signage are all readily adaptable to different shapes and sizes of spaces. To make roll-out economical and feasible, the designer created a few basic pieces which can be added to or subtracted from.

Using a neutral, natural palette of warm, off-white and a honey stained wood, the focal point of the design is the hutch unit with a crown molding on top and cabinet space below cov-

ered with slatted wood doors. The maple colored wood shelves are interrupted by a sign panel which carries the newest promotional ad. Pre-packaged gift items are displayed in the hutch unit which is propped with copper pots, pans and trays, trailing ivy and fresh seasonal plants. To either side of this focal unit, almond colored laminated cases trimmed and edged with light wood are placed. Since there are modular units, the amount used will depend upon the amount of wall space allotted. The area above is slatwall of the same warm almond color and it too is finished with a maple stained crown molding. Blade signs, standing off the wall, clearly indicate where the candy categories can be found.

Rustic provincial farm tables stand out on the floor. Red and white gingham cloths add a splash beneath the merchandise displayed on the table top in natural wood baskets and bushels. Terra cotta pots and red stained wovenwood hampers act as risers and elevations. Surrounding the tables are clusters of small pedestals of assorted heights that support other featured items.

"Our design solutions impacted the overall selling environment without confusing the loyal customer base. The design delivered a new brand message to current customer base and successfully introduced a strong product message to new customers."

DESIGNER ◆ Frankel Brand Environments, Chicago, IL
 Gwen Morrison, VP, Managing Director
 Jim Neill: Design Communications Director
 Ben Oberc: Supervisor of Retail Execution
 Jason Watts & Brendan Nash: Senior Designers
PHOTOGRAPHY ◆ Christopher Barrett, Hedrich Blessing, Ltd., Chicago, IL

THE KITCHENS OF *Fannie May*

fine
chocolates
and
candies
using only
the
freshest
ingredients

THE KITCHENS OF FANNIE MAY

PIXIES

CHOCOLATE
Assortments

FRUIT & NUT
Assortments

TRINIDADS

$11.95
lb.

HAVANNA
Buenos Aires, Argentina

Havanna is Argentina's leading confectioner and also one of that country's most recognized brand names. In order to strengthen its market presence and also gain greater recognition and business volume Havanna contacted Point Design of New York City to implement a new identity program which would include retail environments, signage, stationary, collateral materials and even uniforms and vehicles.

The Havanna Café is a friendly stop-sip-shop spot which combines light refreshments with the aromatic and "sweet tooth" candy experience. At almost any time during the day or evening, the true Argentinian will stop for a relaxing cup of coffee—and a sweet. In the Havanna Café to get to the seating area the patron must pass through the prod-

uct display area which "is quite a powerful impulse area." The 600 sq.ft. area brings it all together in a warm and friendly setting. Deep toned mahogany millwork and cabi-

netry line some of the perimeter walls. On the open, illuminated shelves are the myriad Havanna products in their newly redesigned packaging. The service counters are

finished in the same rich mahogany and they are topped with rust/red laminated counter tops. The same vivid color appears on the terrazzo floor in the service area while in the main seating area the floors are also terrazzo but of a creamier color. One long wall, in the forward coffee area, is papered with a deep apricot color and that is further strengthened by the mural by Martin Jarre filled with reds, blues, yellows, ochers and orange. Yellow walls, with product display, appear the behind the long bar that stretches across most of the space. The concrete columns that support the apricot colored, dropped ceiling over the bar, are streaked with the warm colors as well.

The finely crafted design and the execution of Havanna Café creates a comfortable environment that "builds on the brand's rich heritage."

DESIGNER ◆ Point Design, New York, NY
PROJECT TEAM ◆ Diego Garay, AIA & Luis Bruno: Creative Directors
DESIGNERS ◆ Martin Saens/Leo Lotpolsky/Daniel Solessio
GRAPHIC DESIGN ◆ Derick Hudspith with Lola Arenza & Sol Botindari
LIGHTING CONSULTANT ◆ Pablo Pizzaro Lighting
MILLWORK/CABINETRY ◆ Walsco Construction/Silme/Taddei Equipment
REFRIGERATED CASES ◆ Hobart
MURAL ◆ Martin Jarre, Paris
PHOTOGRAPHY ◆ Gustavo Sosa Pihilla